Ruby Ann's
Down Home Trailer Park
BBQin' Cookbook

Ruby Ann's
Down Home Trailer Park
BBQin' Cookbook

Ruby Ann Boxcar

CITADEL PRESS
Kensington Publishing Corp.
www.kensingtonbooks.com

CITADEL PRESS BOOKS are published by

Kensington Publishing Corp.
850 Third Avenue
New York, NY 10022

All Kensington titles, imprints, and distributed lines are available at special quantity discounts for bulk purchases for sales promotions, premiums, fund-raising, educational, or institutional use. Special book excerpts or customized printings can also be created to fit specific needs. For details, write or phone the office of the Kensington special sales manager: Kensington Publishing Corp., 850 Third Avenue, New York, NY 10022, attn: Special Sales Department, phone 1-800-221-2647.

CITADEL PRESS and the Citadel logo are Reg. U.S. Pat. & TM Off.

The following are trademarks of their respective owners, who do not endorse this book: A&W, A.1., Armway, Avon, Cap'n Crunch, Clorox, Cool Whip, Crisco, Dr Pepper, Dream Whip, Everclear, Frosted Flakes, Fruity Pebbles, Heinz 57 Sauce, Hershey's, Hot Damn, Jell-O, Karo, M&M's, Mary Kay, Mountain Dew, Old Milwaukee, Prestone, Raid, Ritz, Scotch, Shaklee, Skin So Soft, Southern Comfort, Spam, Spirit Foam, Sprite, Styrofoam, Tabasco, Tang, Tupperware, Welch's, Windex, Worcestershire

First printing: May 2003

10 9 8 7 6 5 4 3 2 1

Printed in the United States of America

Library of Congress Control Number: 2002116046

ISBN 0-8065-2536-3

To my sister, Donna Sue
—Eat my dust, darlin'

Contents

Preface

What Does the Word *BBQ* Mean in a Trailer Park?

It's a party—"We're havin' a BBQ in honor of Grandma's release from prison, and was wonderin' if you wanted to come over."

Something you do to your food—"Well I'm sorry about your autographed Barnaby Jones picture, but you can't expect me to BBQ you a few slices of pimiento loaf and watch your momma while she's cleanin' her gun all at the same time. Hell, I ain't Wonder Woman."

A type of sauce—"Would you be kind enough to swat them flies off the BBQ sauce and pass it my way?"

A type of beatin'—"I'm gonna BBQ your hide, boy, if you don't get that spoon out of your mouth and put it back in the potato salad so the rest of us can get some!"

The grill that you use—"All right, doggone it, who peed in the BBQ?"

A food item—"When you get done scratchin', would you please put a handful of that BBQ on my plate?"

Acknowledgments

Thanks to the whole gang at Citadel/Kensington: Walter and Steve Zacharius, Laurie Parkin, Bruce Bender, Joan Schulhafer, Mary Pomponio, Doug Mendini, Lynn Grady, Kris Noble, Michaela Hamilton, and Margaret Wolf.

I also have to acknowledge my husband, Dew, the Good Lord Above (still the Baptist one), and many thanks to my assistant Kevin Wiley for always makin' sure that my hair and makeup look great when I'm doin' a photo shoot, a public appearance, or an all-you-can-eat buffet; to Wiley Designs for takin' my inspiration and puttin' it into clothes, purses, and jewelry; to all those bookstores and their wonderful staffs that recommend my books to their wonderful customers; to all the people in the media that I've come to know over the last year; to all the escorts who drive me around town when I'm in their cities; to the folks at the airport who now or will in the future always find me a better seat; to my drunken sister, Donna Sue, for standin' close to me when we're in public, makin' me look even sexier; to everybody at the High Chaparral Trailer Park; to my family; and to my loyal fans.

Introduction

Hello, friends and fans! The queen of trailer park cuisine, Ruby Ann Boxcar, here with another cookbook that's bound to fill your life with more joy and good eatin' than a person should legally be allowed to have! This time around, the trailer park food topic is BBQin'.

BBQin' is about as common in a trailer park as a visit from the cops. The good Lord in heaven knows that the taste of BBQ can only be beat by the tender lovin' from one's spouse. With that said, it might be why my neighbors BBQ daily. Heck, sometimes they got the fires goin' all day long! As y'all know, nothin' is as captivatin' as the aroma of somethin' cookin' on a grill, with the exception of the winter my sister's dryer broke and she tried to dry out her one-night stand's stockin' cap, which he'd dropped in the snow, by puttin' it on her hibachi. I tell y'all, I don't know what that fella used on his hair, but from the stench that was comin' off his knitted head protector, I know for sure it wasn't Aqua Net or VO 5. You can't imagine! Lord it smelt like somebody was cookin' a mixture of sour milk, hair, and hamburger meat that had expired back in 1969! The newsfolks said people as far up as the southeastern tip of Kansas had complained about the smell. Oh, I'm tellin' y'all it was *bad*. We made her bury that hibachi six feet under to rid the trailer park of the lingerin' odor, but soon we were diggin' it back up on account of how that smell had gotten into our water supply. None of us bathed for a week due to the reekin' water that was comin' out of our faucets, and we still smelled better than the water did. Needless to say, after we dug that dang thing up, the water went back to normal. Donna Sue's hibachi ended up bein' shipped to Mexico via one of them dangerous chemical trucks, her one-night stand is servin' time in jail for murder (he probably killed the poor person by usin' his hairbrush), and my sister is not allowed to BBQ anything without first gettin' permission from the management of the High Chaparral Trailer Park and the state of Arkansas.

Now, before we get started, there are a few things that we need to get straight. First off, when we talk about BBQ we ain't as specific as some folks out there tend to be. In a trailer park, BBQin' can be done with a grill or a smoker. It don't matter to us. Some think that BBQin' and grillin' are two different things. Once again, we don't care. There're those who will tell you that it ain't real BBQ unless it's meat that you're cookin'. Do we look like that matters to us? Others will even insist that BBQ is only when beef has been used. That too don't concern us at all—so start up the dang fire.

There are only two important rules about BBQin' to the folks down at the High Chaparral and they are

1. That you make enough for all of us (if this ain't possible on account of your financial situation, then prepare at least enough for you, your next-door neighbors, and, if I don't fall into that category, me).
2. Your meat is store-bought or caught in a stream (there ain't no exceptions to this rule *ever*).

Actually there is also a third rule at the High Chaparral. If you've read my other books you'll understand it, and if you haven't, well, then you might want to pick up a copy.

3. Never eat what Me-Ma has BBQ'd (*ever*).

Enough said.

As with my prior cookbooks, *Ruby Ann's Down Home Trailer Park Cookbook* and *Ruby Ann's Down Home Trailer Park Holiday Cookbook*, I've gathered all the recipes from my family and neighbors who all live at the High Chaparral Trailer Park in Pangburn, Arkansas. Now that ain't to say that we came up with these tasty food items or that we're the masterminds behind 'em. All it means is that these are the recipes that we all use at the

High Chaparral. And bein' the star and world traveler that I am, I know that most of these same recipes are used every day at trailer parks across the globe. What does that mean for you? Well, not a heck of a lot actually. But I can tell you that me and my sister and the rest of the High Chaparral Trailer Park gang didn't get to look the way we do by eatin' BBQ tofu off of the grill. So the food items you find in this here book have gained the official Ruby Ann Boxcar Seal of Good Eatin'. That means that you can prepare any dish in this book, with the exceptions of those my Me-Ma gave me (please don't make them, since the only reason they made it to print was to make an old senile woman happy), and know full well that they are sure to please all who taste 'em. Now mind you, these recipes ain't magical spells. If you don't like fish, then don't expect to follow a fish recipe, put it on a grill, tap the grill cover three times with your tongs, and have it taste like beef. It's still goin' to taste like fish unless, of course, you happen to be BBQin' over at Lance Burton's house. OK? Good!

Oh, you know there is another thing I should mention that y'all will notice as you continue to read. In my past recipes, when they had cheese in 'em, I put Government cheese and told y'all that if you don't get it, then you could use somethin' else like Cheddar, Swiss, American, or Velveeta for that matter, if you got that kind of money. Well, I just found out recently that Government cheese ain't as easy to get as it used to be. As a matter of fact, I was shocked to learn that there are some places in the United States where you can't even get Government cheese at all. Needless to say, my heart sank all the way down with disbelief. I can't imagine a trailer or even an old home that ain't got a slab of government-approved cheese, which even the mice won't touch. So anyways, I've decided to go ahead and try to find cheese that can replace the U.S.-issued stuff in all the followin' recipes. And for you folks out there who still can get that special-blended government-issued cheese, just use it instead of what's in the recipe. The last thing I want is for somebody to go out and try to shoplift a box of Velveeta from the grocery store. Not only is it wrong, it also means the store has to charge more for groceries—so I got to pay more money so you can have fancy cheese. Well, that ain't gonna work. You don't need to go to hell for stealin', and I don't need to pay an extra $1.50 for a pack of gum, a box of Little Debbie's, or two cans of spray cheese to spread on my

Ritz crackers. Just use the stuff God and Uncle Sam have done already gave you.

Now that we know just where we're comin' from, it's time to get ready for what is truly an American pastime regardless of where you live or what you live in. Get that Hi-Liter™ or pencil and let's move on to the first chapter, 'cause I don't know about you, but my big old bottom is ready to commence with the story-tellin' *and* cookin'!

Update

I asked Momma to give me a photo so I could show y'all how bad that toupee looks on Daddy, and this is what she gave me. If y'all read the Thanksgivin' story in my *Holiday Cookbook,* then this is a double treat for you, since it was taken on that terrible day by my husband, Dew, while he was holdin' his breath.

The Residents of the High Chaparral Trailer Park, Lot by Lot

Since we last talked, lots of things have happened at and around the High Chaparral Trailer Park. We've had a few folks leave us both willingly and unwillingly. We've also had a few new folks move in and join our little community of God-fearin', flag-wavin', proud-to-live-in-a-trailer-park Americans. Another business fire has affected one of us, while another resident is waitin' for his new business to finish bein' built. A new craze has found its way into our little corner of the world, as did a freakish tornado that touched down and took a trailer. We've got a new place for the families to enjoy, and a pastor who wishes she got a Dell. And all that just barely scratches the surface of what we call "livin'" at the twenty-lot High Chaparral Trailer Park.

By the way, folks, as some of y'all know who've either seen me durin' my book tours or visited my Web pages at www.rubyann.org, we folks at the First Baptist Church of Pangburn have been in search of a name change. You see, we've been gettin' lots of flak about the disposition of our now former Pastor Richard Hickey, which y'all will recall my mentionin' in *Ruby Ann's Down Home Trailer Park Holiday Cookbook*. And even though we got a new minister, Pastor Ida May Bee, we were still havin' people stop by the church lookin' to get a view of Pastor Hickey. And the telephone calls were just as bad, if not worse. Folks would call the church at all times of the day askin' to speak with "Teeny Wienie Hickey," "Father Finger-long," "Reverend Small Stuff," "Minister No Thrill," or "Pastor Dick Less," and those were just the halfway clever ones that we got (now that last one made more sense, since his first name was Richard). It was just terrible, and it got to the point to where nobody wanted to answer the church phone. But that wasn't that half of it. You should have seen the way people treated us when we attended Baptist functions with other churches. Why, you couldn't have gotten a Unitarian to say some of the names these folks were callin' us behind our backs and right to our faces. I mean, it was bad. So we decided at first to just put up big signs outside the church that said HE AIN'T HERE! And when we answered the church phone instead of sayin', "Thank you for callin' the First Baptist Church of Pangburn," we'd start off with, "He ain't here, First Baptist Church of Pangburn, thank you for callin'." Well, that didn't go over real well, and now we had people goin' around sayin' that the "he" in HE AIN'T HERE was God. So folks now thought we weren't holy. Plus, there were rumors goin' around that we were passin' out snakes durin' our services, that we no longer had potlucks, and that when we did we were always the last in line 'cause we didn't care about important Baptist traditions like a good homemade casserole dish or an ambrosia salad. It was just all lies. So we decided to change our name. We had a church meetin' and came up with ten names that we really liked. The church printed 'em up and I took 'em with me on all my travels, askin' people to pick their favorite one. I also let the church link to my Web pages so folks could vote online for their favorite new name selection. Those choices were

Bible Belt Baptist Church (It kind of says it all.)

By the Bay Baptist Church (Sister Bertha wanted seagulls and sailboats painted on the baptismal wall.)

First in Line Baptist Church (To the point.)

First in the Gate Baptist Church (The gate we was talkin' about was the pearly one, not the one at the Golden Coral, The Sizzler, or any other cafeteria-type restaurant where you get a tray and stand in the gated section, although that would have been fine as well.)

Holier Than Most Baptist Church (That'll teach 'em.)

Hope You Make It Baptist Church (Don't worry about us, but watch your step.)

No Snakes in Here Baptist Church (Heck, I can't even watch 'em on TV.)

Razorback Baptist Church (Go Pig!)

The Back Door Baptist Church (The front door was broken at the time so you
had to use the back door.)

Turn the Light on Baptist Church (Hey, somethin' like this worked real well for
a popular motel, so we didn't see where it could hurt.)

Those were your choices and accordin' to Lovie and Elmer Birch who
officiated the count, the new name of the First Baptist Church of
Pangburn is . . .

Holier Than Most Baptist Church!

Thank you all so much for your time and your votes. Make sure you
stop by my Web pages at www.rubyann.org 'cause you never know when
we might need y'all to vote on somethin' else in the near future.

LOT #1

This September will mark the first weddin' anniversary of Pangburn's own
dirt-ugly Opal Lamb and her attractive, yet catty husband, Dick Inman. It
still amazes all of us at the High Chaparral Trailer Park that dear unattractive Opal was able to land a man, especially one who still has his sight. But
I guess they're happy. Accordin' to Opal, her and Dick have nothin' but
pure bliss. When Opal goes to bed at night, her thoughtful husband, who
knows she has to get up early in the mornin' to open Lamb Department
Store, waits until she's fallen completely asleep before he comes to bed.

Dick has started practicin' law again. As many of you might recall, he
moved back here from California where he had a practice. He's rentin' out
a buildin' in Pangburn from my niece, Lulu Bell, but is workin' out of his
trailer until the remodelin' is finished. Lulu Bell says he really is makin' it
fancy and all. He has a nice little waitin' area where his secretary will have
her desk, and then his office, which sets directly behind her, is real pretty
with beautiful wood panelin'. Accordin' to Lulu Bell, he's even puttin' in a
special little section in the back of the buildin' for his clients to use. It has
a steam room, Jacuzzi area, locker and shower section, and a movie room.
Dick has also thought about how some of the people goin' through a messy
divorce, whose cases he'll be handlin', may not have a lot of money to

spend on a motel room, so he's put in these little numbered small rooms with just enough space for a cot and a mounted wall TV. Say what you want about most lawyers, but that Dick Inman, I'll tell you, that man's got a good heart, that's for sure.

As far as he and Opal's live-in maid goes, it was nothin' but drama. Fernando Diaz (he's only eighteen) was arrested around Thanksgivin' and deported back to Mexico for usin' a fake visa to gain entry into the U.S. The funny part was that just the night before, Kenny and Donny had gotten into a big argument with both Dick and Fernando down by the mailboxes. There was a lot of yellin' and hollerin' and we all think it had somethin' to do with Kenny and Donny's fervent campaign against cock fightin', or at least that's what it sounded like what they was sayin'. With the wind blowin' like it was, it was hard to make out all the words. Needless to say, both Opal and Dick were shocked and put out an ad in the *Bugle* sayin' how sorry they were about bringin' an illegal alien into our community. They swore they had no idea that he wasn't legal or that he was wanted in Texas on fraud charges, where he'd lived under the name of Maria Conchita Sanchez.

Dick was extremely upset with the deportation of Fernando, and can you blame him? With the busy life he and Opal live, who's got time to cook and clean their trailer? So later that night after they hauled Fernando away, Dick went to Little Rock and came back later in the week with a new live-in Russian maid and a butler. Uri Krochichin (also eighteen) and Buck N. Hiney (he's nineteen) share Fernando's old room, but Dick replaced Fernando's full-size bed with a king-size so they could have plenty of room. When asked why they didn't just get each of 'em a twin bed, Dick said it would've cost more to get two twin-size beds than it did to just get one king.

LOT #2

An early-mornin' fire, which started in recently opened Leroy Johnson's Thai One On Restaurant spread over to the adjoinin' Three Cigarettes in the Ashtray Bar and Grill, burnin' both them and one of the other businesses in the strip mall down to the ground. Of course, none of us had been to Leroy's restaurant, so that wasn't a real loss, but the destruction of Anita Biggon's bar nearly tore our hearts out. Oh, it was just a tragedy, 'cause they had some of the best dang food in town. Luckily they were able to get most of the valuable items out of Anita's place on account of an early warnin' system, Leroy Johnson, who was asleep in the office above his restaurant. As soon as them flames stated lickin' at the underside of the cot he was a snoozin' on, he jumped up and out the second-story window.

He called the sheriff, who in turn contacted The House of Holes Donut Hut and had 'em set aside two of their old-fashioneds and a glazed twist, since he was most likely goin' to be late gettin' in, Anita Biggon at her trailer home, and the head of the volunteer fire department, all in that order. Well, Anita in return called Kyle Chittwood, since he bartends at the joint and told him to throw some clothes on and meet her down there. As he headed out the door, his wife, Kitty, called me and my husband, Dew, Mickey Ray Kaye, Harland Hix, and several of the other folks in the trailer park to see if we could rush over to the bar and help Anita and Kyle save whatever wasn't nailed down. Of course, we all jumped up and rushed over to the Three Cigarettes in the Ashtray to do our Christian duties, and as you can guess, I put my makeup on first. We arrived about ten minutes later than the rest of the folks, and the bar was nearly gone, but even at that time in the mornin', in the glowin' light of a three-alarm fire, I got to tell y'all, I looked doggone good. But my appearance, no matter how attractive, was no condolence to those weepin' around me.

Poor Anita had lost her bar, Leroy Johnson's dreams had gone up in flames, and Sister Bertha, dressed in a big faded blue terrycloth house robe and fuzzy slippers, was one big puddle of tears. Not use to seein' her sobbin' like she was, I ran to Sister Bertha to see if she was all right. After all, I knew she wasn't cryin' because the bar had burnt down. To her that place was nothin' more than "the devil's tavern," and she'd said so on many occasions. And I know her uncontrollable cryin' wasn't due to the loss of Leroy Johnson's Thai restaurant, since neither her or anyone else other than my sister and some of the gals at the Blue Whale had ever eaten there (nobody except them around these parts really gets into all that bondage stuff). So what could've upset poor Sister Bertha so bad? Well, it didn't take much time to solve that mystery. Just as soon as I'd reached her, she looked up, wiped away some of her tears with her soggy tissue, and said, "Oh, Ruby Ann, they weren't able to save the pickles." I'd forgotten how much she loved those fried pickles that they served. Y'all might recall in my holiday cookbook how I mentioned her cunnin' schemes that she'd pull on folks just to get 'em to go down to the bar and pick her up an order of pickles. Anita came over and assured her that they could always order more pickles and that they had managed to save the recipe for the batter. After hearing that, Sister Bertha jumped up and quietly threw her arms around Anita. For just a moment on that terrible early mornin' there it was as if they'd bonded.

I've got to tell you how proud I was of the folks from the trailer park who came and helped. Not only were they not afraid to jump right in to help a neighbor, but the ways they came up to fight off the flames while they waited for the volunteer fire department to arrive was pure genius. Kenny and Donny from Lot # 15 were quick enough on their feet to run across the street to the Suck and Squirt Car Wash, pop in a few quarters, and start sprayin' powerful streams of water on the burnin' buildin's. I couldn't believe how good both Kenny and Donny were with those long high-pressured rods. Of course, Lulu Bell had to continue feedin' quarters that she'd ran and got from her nearby business, Lulu Bell's Pool Hall, into the car wash money box ever few minutes or Kenny and Donny would quickly dry up. And then there was Dottie Lamb and Ben Beaver. I have no idea where they came up with the idea to tie a rope to the back of Ben's wheelchair and then push him into the flickerin' flames armed with nothin' more then a wet blanket and a will to live. As soon as he'd give the word, Dottie would pull him back out of the fire by the attached rope. They'd quickly have the boys shoot their hoses on Ben and his smolderin' blanket, and then Dottie would push him back into the growin' inferno. Thanks to those two, they were able to keep the roarin' flames away from the front door of Anita's place so the rest of the gang could bring a lot of the items out. I'm sure even more could have been saved if only that rope hadn't burnt clean through. Kenny and Donny had to hose down Opal from ugly head to toe just so she could bravely run in and pull Ben and his wheelchair out. When I spoke to Opal later to congratulate her on how heroic she'd been runnin' into that burnin' buildin' and all, she said she was just fine, but I bet that somebody could have sent in a photo of her to the insurance company and they'd have paid a lot of money to settle real quick, if you know what I mean.

Long story short, both Leroy and Anita had insurance, so they were fine. The reason for the fire was blamed on old wiring in those buildin's, and the fella who owned the property decided not to do any rebuildin' just yet. We told Leroy that if he decided to reopen a restaurant, he ought to go with something Asian this time around. We could use a place nearby that served some good Asian food. To tell you the truth, I don't think Leroy really cared what we thought, 'cause he just stood there lookin' at us like we were stupid or somethin'.

Within a month's time, Anita had laid a concrete foundation and put up a metal buildin' down by the highway. And quickly there after Anita's Bar and Grill was opened up for business. She even added a drive-thru around the back of the buildin' so more discreet folks could drive up for food orders . . . like fried pickles and such.

As for the third business that burnt, well, it was a little gift shop that had been around for years. It was owned and run by this little elderly Mennonite woman who always had a big basket of cookies that she'd baked that mornin' to give out to everyone who came through her door regardless if they made a purchase or not. Everyone called her Granny, and she was one of the kindest souls you'd ever meet. She did, however, refuse to carry any of my books 'cause she thought I was wearin' too much makeup in the pictures on the book covers. The poor dear thing didn't have a lick of insurance and lost everything. Pity!

LOT #3

Business sure was saggin' at the new Taco Tackle Shack North just a month after it's big openin'. Poor Lois and Hubert Bunch, who live in Lot #3, were just puzzled at why this was so. After all, they were servin' all the same great-tastin' Tex-Mex food items as well as stockin' all the same fine-quality fishin' gear and bait that they carried just a block away at their original

Taco Tackle Shack location. And to make matters worse, that Taco Tackle Shack was still bringin' 'em in. As a matter of fact, their business hadn't changed a bit. So what were they to do? Well, I suggested that maybe people were still comin' to the original location 'cause on account of it bein' where Lois and Hubert were at. With that in mind, Lois went down to the Taco Tackle Shack North while Hubert manned the register at the other Taco Tackle Shack. Sure enough, business went up at the north store, but it dropped by 50 percent at the south location, which meant that with the income of both stores combined, they was still makin' the same amount of money they'd made with just one business location. It looked like they were just gonna have to close down one of the stores.

Lois and Hubert were doin' OK financially thanks to the steady income of the Fisherman's Friend, which y'all will recall is a little tiny drive-up hut over by the highway where folks can get a coffee and a sweet roll along with their fishin' supply needs on their way to their favorite spot at the lake, pond, or river. But of course the Bunches were extremely stressed-out and frustrated on account of this whole second store dilemma. So I invited 'em to come up to Commerce City, Colorado, where y'all know me and my husband, Dew, keep our quad-wide holiday trailer home (they wouldn't let us build up with a second story like we did in Pangburn, so we built out). I thought a get-away from the situation might help 'em to think, and if not, well at least I knew I'd be eatin' good with Lois in my kitchen.

When my husband, Dew, drove us all around so I could show 'em neighborin' Denver, the Bunches were just shocked at all the wonderful Mexican restaurants that we had to choose from. That was when I told 'em that if they wanted to see somethin' unique, they had to go to a little place called Casa Bonita. This place is decorated to resemble a Mexican village at night, and they even have a cave, and a waterfall that runs down these cliffs and into a deep pool area. But of course me and my husband, Dew, go there on account of it bein' all you can eat. Well, needless to say, both Lois and Hubert were inspired, of course not enough to change their format to an all-you-can-eat one. When they got back to Pangburn, Lois and Hubert went crazy and ran a $100 ad campaign advertisin' what would turn out to be a weekly craze. Every Wednesday and Thursday night between eight and ten, the Taco Tackle Shack North would feature cliff divers just like they do at Denver's own Casa Bonita. Well, you should have seen the line of people that ran out the door come eight o'clock on that first Wednesday night. The place was packed and folks were waitin' to get in. Lois was slingin' that food like a crazy woman, and the stink bait and night crawlers were flyin' out the door. And all of this on account of one little trip to Denver, where Lois and Hubert got their first taste of indoor cliff divin'. Of course, the show you get at the Taco Tackle Shack North ain't exactly what you'll see at Casa Bonita. After all, Casa Bonita has a towerin' thirty-foot-high waterfall with brave fire-baton-twirlin' divers. The show at the Bunches' restaurant and fishin' supplies consists of three midgets jumpin' off of a chair into a turtle pool with disposable lighters in their hands. It ain't quite as death defyin', but, boy, I'll tell you, it sure is fun to watch. And if that garden hose they got duct taped to the seat of the chair don't kink up, the sound of that water flowin' into the turtle pool along with the smell of Lois's enchantin' Tex-Mex cuisine makes you feel like you've been whisked away to a Mexican local. As you can guess, once word spread after that first show, Thursday night was even busier. Why, this has become so trendy that Pastor Ida May Bee now holds the Wednesday night service over at the Holier Than Most Baptist Church from 6:00 to 7:45 P.M., and then she joins the rest of the attendin' congregation over at the Taco Tackle Shack North, where retired minister Hubert Bunch holds a special reserved table for her and her husband, Brother Woody Bee.

Last I checked, come Wednesday and Thursday, there ain't an empty seat in the north location. And don't quote me on this, but with the boom in business that the Bunches are havin', rumor has it that they've been spotted at the Wal-Mart lookin' at turtle pools. Could it be that a show is in the works for the original restaurant as well?

LOT #4

When it comes to handlin' an organ, I thought no one was as good at it as my stripper sister, Donna Sue (she used to back me from time to time on the Hammond), but I was wrong. Nellie Tinkle has shown that there ain't no organ too big or small for her nimble fingers. And you should see what she can do with her feet! As many of y'all know, Nellie has been the organist at my church for years. Just last December she asked to take a short sabbatical so that she could devote some time to her new organ-tunin' business, which has been a lifelong dream of hers come true. And as y'all will recall, Nellie and her husband, C.M., allowed ninety-year-old widow Wendy Bottom to move into the spare bedroom at Lot #4 so she could learn how to play the organ, thus takin' over for Nellie when she's off blowin' organs with her new company, Nellie's Tinklin' Organ. Dear old sweet Wendy is real nice and all, but still there was rumor and innuendo that while Nellie was away, the church organ, which has been looked upon by all who attend services at the Holier Than Most Baptist Church as her own, was goin' to be taken over by Wendy. Well, this was just idiotic, I can assure you. Try as hard as she may to do a good job on the keyboard, Wendy, God bless her, is not a Nellie Tinkle. Trust me when I tell y'all that Nellie's organ will not be easily "owned," as some folks like to say, by anyone who plays a hymn with one finger at a time. That's right, dear reader, you can be sure that Nellie's organ has nothin' to fear from a Wendy Bottom.

With all rumors aside, what I was tryin' to get to was the fact that when it came to organ playin', the only type of music that most of us have heard Nellie play was from the Baptist hymnal or old traditional standbys, which she'd entertain us with at other non-church related events. So you can imagine our surprise when we got to hear Nellie workin' the keyboard and foot pedals to newer secular tunes. You see, she got called in to tune the organ at the newly opened Rinky Dink Roller Rink out by the highway (see Lot #9). It seemed that the new rink couldn't use records or CDs to play their skatin' music on account of where it was located. Unbeknownst to the owners, the property that the rink sat on wasn't actually part of Pangburn, so it fell under a different set of rules and laws. One of those laws, which dates back to the early 1920s, don't allow the playin' of recorded music or any other kind of music played by an instrument other than an organ in a place of business. This was done so that gin joints, speakeasies, or dance clubs at the time couldn't open up in that area of the state, but places of worship, which'd typically use an organ, could. And of course, just like every other state in the Union, this was one of those old laws that, even though outdated, had not been stricken from the books. Anyways, long story short, they had to have an organ if they was goin' to have music. So they got an old movie-theater pipe organ over at the Real Easy Pawn and hired on Nellie to get it into workin' condition. Needless to say, she got that organ singin' like magic. As a matter of fact, she had it soundin' so good that they hired her to come in when they're open on Friday and Saturday nights and play. You ain't heard nothin' till you've heard Nellie's boogie-woogie version of the "Hokey Pokey." Why, with the way she tinkles on the organ, I wouldn't be surprised if roller boogie don't make a comeback in the Pangburn area in the very near future. I hear that even as I put pen to paper, she's workin' on a stirrin' organ rendition of Olivia Newton-John's classic "Xanadu." Heck, I think I'd be helpless to the temptation of strappin' on a pair of skates and bustin' my bottom along with the floorboards if she does work up that particular number.

LOT #5

I do not know what kind of demon has possessed my dear sweet daddy now age seventy-seven, but he's decided to wear a toupee. God bless him, the man was bald-head by the time he turned twenty-four. He ain't had nothin' but patches of wispy hair around the sides of his head since before I was a baby and now he thinks that after all these years he needs a hairpiece. A hat, yes, a comb-over, maybe, but a hairpiece, no. And I'm thinkin' the same demon that's got a hold of Daddy must of jumped into Momma (she's seventy-three) as well, 'cause she ain't sayin' nothin' to discourage this insanity. And to make matters worse, that thing he's wearin' on his head has got to be the ugliest piece of matted, unnatural synthetic material that's ever touched a scalp since Captain James T. Kirk boarded the *Enterprise*. Why, the poor man fell asleep outside his trailer durin' a recent BBQ, and when he woke up a squirrel had climbed up on top of that thing and commenced to matin'. By the time he got that furry little critter (the squirrel, not his toupee) off his head there were nuts everywhere. I tell you folks, it ain't right, and it sure don't look right either.

LOT #6

Donna Sue, (who recently turned fifty-seven) has decided to branch out from the wonderful world of exotic dancin' and has opened her own business. Don't think for a minute that this means she's stopped or even cut back on her work as the headliner at the Blue Whale Strip Club. No, we couldn't be that lucky. But what she has done is opened her own pawnshop, called Real Easy Pawn, and may I say that even though I had my doubts, it's a hit. You should see all the junk she's got down there. When she say's she'll give you a top-dollar loan on anythin' you're willin' to pawn, she means it. Of course considerin' the hours she keeps, and the fact that she's the only employee at the store, you really never know when the place is open. She don't post no business times, but people don't seem to mind since they know that once she is open for business, at the pawnshop that is, it's well worth their wait. And not only does she pay you well, she sells the stuff real cheap too. That's on account of the fact that the buildin' is yet another property that's owned by my niece, Lulu Bell. In return for the use of the buildin', she has let Lulu Bell use her spare key and take whatever she wants. That means that if there is a Billy Ray Cyrus or Kathy Lee Gifford CD or tape in the store, it's hers. Other than that, Lulu Bell really ain't all that interested. Of course, me and Momma and Daddy told Donna Sue that she should at least give Lulu Bell $100 a month, which she agreed to. Of course, she also sent Lulu Bell and her boyfriend, Billy Bob, to Walt Disney World and Universal Studios in Florida as a way of sayin' thanks. But other than the small rent and the utilities bill (how much can it cost to have the lights on twelve hours a week), she ain't got hardly any overhead to take care of. So she only marks stuff up 10 or 15 percent more than what she gave for it. Her merchandise goes flyin' out of that store. She has to be makin' a killin'. I tell you, folks, my sister ain't dumb. Why she's just started up an ad campaign that's got 'em comin' from as far up as Little Rock. It consists of a photo of her dressed in a tube top and a pair of slacks that are so tight the strings are cryin' in pain, surrounded by the stuff in her store. At the bottom of the ad it gives the store address and right above it in big words is her store motto, "Hi, I'm Donna Sue, and I'm Real Easy!" You be surprised at how many folks show up not knowin' it's a pawn store.

Anyways, she's talkin' about branchin' out into some other new business as well, but I'm not sure about that one. All I know is it might involve a cart, a donkey, and a pair of tongs, which scares the heck out of me.

LOT #7

This past Christmas everyone in the church got together and pitched in on a special present for our beloved Pastor Ida May Bee and her husband, Brother Woody Bee. Knowin' that they both like a good meal, the whole congregation accompanied Pastor Ida May Bee and Brother Woody Bee over to Wally's Noodle Hut in neighborin' Heber Springs. When it comes to great Italian food, nobody does it like Wally Chang. He's got the best sweet-and-sour manicotti that I've ever had, not to mention his fantastic wonton biscotti. And the cannoli fortune cookies are to die for! Pastor Ida May Bee gave the sesame chicken cacciatore three hanky waves and two "amens." And then after the dinner we presented Pastor Ida May Bee with a gift we knew she could really use. You see, unlike Pastor Hickey, who hardly ever left his house other than for church services, Pastor Ida May Bee is always on the go. Every mornin' she visits the sick and needy. Once a week she goes over to the Last Stop Nursing Home to pray with the sick. She is always in the "go" mode, so to speak. So we folks thought what would be better than a laptop that she could use in the car while Brother Woody Bee drives her to the next destination. So that night before the fine Italian cuisine, Sister Bertha made a presentation to the Bees and gave them a gift certificate for a laptop. We wanted to wait until we'd had our dinner to see how much money we had so we could get her the best model possible. Well, needless to say, when the check came we just about threw a disk. Who would have thought that thirty-eight people could have eaten $114.67 worth of food! I guess that's what you can expect to pay when you go to a fancy eatin' place. 'Course, there was no way we could get even a good used laptop for $200! So Sister Bertha was forced to go online to one of them auction sites and try to find somethin'. I can only assume she prayed before firin' up her Dell, 'cause within just hours Sister Bertha had pieced together a computer system and had it on its way to the High

Chaparral Trailer Park. You should have seen the look on Pastor Ida May Bee's face when we all gathered outside her trailer and presented her with her new mobile computer. Well, the mouse was new at least. The actual terminal was a 1973 model that some college in Oklahoma was sellin' off. After Brother Woody Bee had moved the spare tire to the front seat, the terminal fit nicely into the trunk with just enough space for the hood to close almost all the way. And the monitor took up less than half the back-seat on the driver's side. When Pastor Ida May Bee was positioned just right on the passenger's side in the backseat, she actually had room for the keyboard. Needless to say, she was just thrilled to tears. The Bible's right, sometimes it truly is better to give than it is to receive.

LOT #8

After actually watchin' with my own eyes dear old unattractive Opal Lamb-Inman walk down the aisle as a bride last year, the news that my simple-minded niece, Lulu Bell (she's thirty-four now), is goin' steady with a boy don't throw me at all. With all the heartache that gal has had to go through, includin' the abandonment from her hateful witch of a mother, Blanche, and the untimely accident death of her daddy, I wish nothin' but happiness for her. She's taken that money that she inherited, and she's turned it into a gold mine. She bought that pool hall and has it goin' real good, plus she purchased all that land and has been rentin' or resellin' it like crazy. Even though she's one shoe short of a sale, if you know what I mean, she's turned out to be the Leona Helmsley of the High Chaparral Trailer Park, without all that jail time of course. And I sure am proud of her.

This new boyfriend, Billy Bob Buttons (he's her exact same age), has done pretty good for himself as well. As a matter of fact, he bought the old Dirty Drive Car Wash with the money he'd saved since childhood by sellin' *Grit* magazine. He went in there and added new state-of-the-art high-tech vacuums and the latest-model high-pressure sprayin' wands. And I got to tell y'all that for my money, Billy Bob's Suck and Squirt Car Wash is one of the best outside of Little Rock. But don't think that Billy Bob is all work.

Far from it, accordin' to Lulu Bell, who as y'all recall nearly killed him in the last book on Valentine's Day. When Lulu Bell hangs out with him at the Suck and Squirt he keeps sneakin' up behind her with those vacuum hoses and attachin' 'em to her neck when she ain't lookin'. I swear, sometimes she comes home with more marks on her neck than her aunt Donna Sue does.

Billy Bob and Lulu Bell ain't set a date yet, they're waitin' on the state to say they can marry, which shouldn't really be a problem, but I do know he loves her. And when you ask Billy Bob what he likes most about Lulu Bell, he says he loves her smile, her wit, her laugh, and the way that she don't wear a bra around the trailer. Oh, young love!

LOT #9

After what has been a terrible time in their lives, it finally looks like the sun is about to peek out from behind the clouds. For those of you who ain't heard it yet, around the end of December Harland Hix (age thirty-one) was struck in the head by a wild bowlin' ball. He was sprayin' down the shoes behind the counter when all of a sudden from out of nowhere a ball came flyin' through the air and smacked him right upside the noggin. Accordin' to our town paper, the *Bugle*, the ball had come off the hand of ninety-six-year-old bowler Esther Higgins durin' an attempt to pick up a split. Luckily for Harland the ball was only a seven-pounder, which is unusually light for an adult's ball. It was, however, heavy enough to keep Harland in intensive care for three days in the hospital over in Searcy. The side of his head was swelled up like half a giant pumpkin. As Harland was finally makin' his way back home to be with his wife, Juanita, all the details of the accident publicly emerged. It seems that Esther Higgins, who has a 198 average, slipped in a large puddle on the lane. This puddle was caused from the melted ice that was on the shoes of fellow bowlers. The owner of the Great Big Balls Bowlin' Alley, Casper P. Bowen, had encouraged folks who had to run out to their cars durin' a game to go ahead and wear their bowlin' shoes. Casper's take was that most folks run out to their car 'cause they need more cash or a check so they can buy a drink or food item.

Makin' 'em change their shoes first might make the customers feel that the trip out to the car was just too much of a hassle, so they'd stay inside and skip that drink or food item. Well that little decision of Casper's cost his insurance company $130,000, which poor old pumpkin head Harland was more than happy to accept from the comfort of his wheelchair. With that cash settlement and a month's worth of free bowlin', Harland was able to retire from his job at the Great Big Balls as well as give up his position at the Piggly Wiggly. Harland and Juanita took that money, paid off the hospital bills, and spent the rest in convertin' an old barn down by the highway into the newly opened Rinky Dink Roller Rink. You can just imagine the excitement they both had while creatin' a place that families could come together and laugh, smile, and crack the whip. Juanita is still workin' over at the Piggly Wiggly, but come Friday and Saturday, her place is behind the concession stand at their new rink. The swellin' in Harland's head has gone down quite a bit, and the doctor says that Harland should be back to normal come September of this year.

As for Esther Higgins, she was lucky she wasn't hurt when she slipped. And once they'd wiped the blood from her ball, she went on to claim victory of that split.

LOT #10

Ollie White, sixty-four, is back in the swing with that terrible scandal, which I mentioned in the holiday cookbook, far behind her. This promises to be Ollie's year. She's gearin' up for this year's competition of the Hair Net Award, and as y'all will recall, they're givin' her a lifetime achievement award as well. And of course she's still workin' as head cook at the school cafeteria. Molly Piper is the only gal over her, but Ollie says she can keep that position. Havin' to plan out the week's menu, keep track of stock, and put in orders for food is more work than Ollie wants to handle at her age. Plus she goes on to say that the only reason Molly has that job anyways is 'cause she's havin' an affair with one of the members of the school board. Accordin' to Ollie, Molly Piper is nothin' more than a glorified boy toy whose behavior in the bedroom has garnished her that $1.09-more-an-hour wage. If Ollie wanted to dress up in a tight skirt and a low-cut blouse, paradin' her goods all over town like Molly does, then she could probably have that job as well. Now let me just add right here that I don't know if Ollie is sayin' all this out of jealousy or truth. After all, Molly is eighty-seven years old and uses a walker to get around. On the other hand, she does wear a push-up bra.

LOT #11

Well, thank goodness Kitty Chitwood owns the Gas and Smokes convenience store, or her and her husband, Kyle, would've been in a mess of hurt after that fire destroyed Anita's Three Cigarettes in the Ashtray Bar and Grill. Kyle, as y'all will recall, is nighttime bartender there, and with that place gone, he would have been forced to go out and find other employment until Anita got her new bar goin'. But luckily, thanks to Kitty's business, he could just set at home and wait. Of course that didn't help their marriage much. At first Kitty thought it would be nice comin' home around 5:30 in the evenin' every night and gettin' to spend some time with her husband. Normally they only got Saturday day, and all of Sunday to spend together on account of her havin' both those days off and the Three Cigarettes in the Ashtray bein' closed on Sundays. But with this new schedule, on account of the fire, Kyle was home 24-7. The first week was nice and romantic for Kitty and Kyle. She'd come home, he'd have supper on the TV trays, and then they'd set down together and eat while they watched TV. But by the end of the week things started to take a turn for the worse. Kitty would get mad 'cause right in the middle of *Entertainment Tonight* Kyle would fall asleep. Come *Friends*, he'd be snorin' so loud she couldn't hear the dang TV. She was really gettin' ticked off as the week continued, 'cause after all, he would sleep in until 8:30 or 9:00 A.M. and then fall off before 7:00 P.M. You'd think he could at least stay up until 8:15 or 8:40 P.M., which is about the time she'd doze off on the couch. But luckily it only took 'em about a month and a half to get Anita's Bar and Grill up and goin', and Kyle and Kitty are back to their old selves. She falls asleep watchin' TV by herself durin' the week, and Kyle joins her in slumber-

ville shortly after he gets home from work at around 2:30 in the mornin',
usually with a half-drunk beer in his hand. Paradise has returned to Lot
#11.

LOT #12

I got to be honest, folks, I really thought we was gonna have some trouble
at church between Sister Bertha (age sixty) and our new pastor, Pastor Ida
May Bee, when she took over from former Pastor Hickey last year. I was
certain there'd be a power struggle of some kind, since Sister Bertha is one
of those take-charge kinds of women, if you know what I mean. After all,
it was Sister Bertha and not Pastor Hickey, as y'all might recall, who'd
come bangin' on your trailer door on Sunday night to find out why you
weren't at church. So we were sure that there'd be trouble when another
woman came into the picture, even though that other woman had served
at our church as assistant pastor for the past twelve years. And if Pastor Ida
May Bee hadn't been prepared to handle Sister Bertha and her little group
of self-righteous womenfolk, we might've seen a revolt in our friendly
community. But thank goodness it never happened. You see, the one thing
that Pastor Ida May Bee realized right away, which Pastor Hickey never
thought of, was that if you keep someone like Sister Bertha busy with
other chores in the church, she ain't got a lot of time to do anythin' that'll
cause a problem. And so the first thing Pastor Ida May Bee did was to ap-
point Sister Bertha in charge of the operation of the church bus. As I mentioned in the holiday book, Sister Bertha took to drivin' our little
renovated fourteen-passenger school bus like a duck to water. Speakin' of
water, our pastor also gave her the task of maintainin' the baptismal tank.
Sister Bertha would grab the garden hose and make sure that the water was
at a certain level at all times in the tank. Why she even did chlorine tests to
ensure that when a person was baptized it was both a religious experience
and a healthy one as well. Needless to say, Sister Bertha was kept on her
toes at all times, but those troublemaker followers of hers were not happy.
They wanted to be more in the spotlight, but instead of goin' to Pastor Ida
May Bee themselves, they went runnin' to Sister Bertha. Well, all their

rantin' and ravin' got Sister Bertha all stirred up, so that one Tuesday evenin' she marched her uppity self as well as the other five ticked-off women over to Lot #7 and banged on Pastor Ida May Bee's trailer door, demandin' a meetin' right then and there. Well, Pastor Ida May said of course and welcomed 'em all into her humble abode. After offerin' 'em all a glass of sweet tea, she went on to say how happy she was that they'd all stopped by to see her, 'cause the Lord had laid all of 'em on her heart recently. Before Sister Bertha could say a word, Pastor Ida May Bee said that she wanted to start up a committee that would be in charge of makin' their church a place that God would be happy to hang his hat. It'd basically be a flower committee, where these ladies would come in and arrange the plastic flowers and even buy new ones from time to time. They'd make sure that there was the right amount of donated fans from the funeral home in each seat, as well as at least one box of off-brand tissues in every other pew. It'd be their responsibility to dust off both the Christian flag and United States flag, which proudly stand on each side of the baptismal tank. And of course, they'd make sure that there was always a clean glass, a pitcher of fresh water, and a full bottle of anointin' oil settin' under the pulpit before the start of each service. Accordin' to Pastor Ida May Bee, when she'd finished, all of 'em, includin' Sister Bertha just set there with their mouths open. Oh, I wish I'd been a fly on the wall for that one! Can you imagine the surprise those tired old hags got when Pastor Ida May Bee started talkin' about them makin' up a committee? Pastor Ida May Bee said that the only thing they could do was to agree to serve. And of course quickly vote in Sister Bertha as the committee chair on account of her havin' a spare key to the church already. With that she opened her trailer door and thanked 'em all for comin' over. What she didn't tell 'em was that her husband, Brother Woody Bee, had overheard 'em complainin' inside Sister Bertha's trailer while he was takin' his nightly walk around the High Chaparral. He'd already told his wife what was bein' said before those old bags had even started out to see her, so by the time they knocked on her door, she was prepared for 'em. I tell you, she's a smart one all right, and I'll tell you both Sister Bertha and those on that committee haven't had another bad word to say about Pastor Ida May Bee. They treat her with respect both as a spiritual leader and a woman in the church. I'm sure it's mostly because of the way she treated 'em that night. And of course the fact that later that same night a tornado came and wiped out Sister Bertha's trailer. Don't worry, she was fine. For some reason every time Pastor Ida May Bee tells this story, when she gets to the tornado part, she gets a little smile and a twinkle appears in her eye. You know, now that I think of it, that was the first twister that I recall hittin' in the dead of winter.

LOT #13

Mickey Ray Kay, over in Lot #13 has confirmed to me that Dottie Lamb has asked him to be the manager of the new company that she and her dog-ugly daughter, Opal, are buildin' where the old Lamb Department Store used to stand before it burned down (see Lot #14). This would mean that he'd be leavin' his post as manager over at the Dr Pepper plant. Of course the pay would be good, and even though the new company is sure to be a hit, at this time in the game it'd be like leavin' your job sellin' Cadillacs to go sell GEO Metros. As we go to print on this book, Mickey Ray is still thinkin' and prayin' about it, but I'll keep you updated.

Poor Connie Kay. We love her to death, just as long as she ain't tryin' to push one of her product lines on you. But my heart went out to her durin' this past Christmas parade. You see, she thought it would be fun if she walked the short parade route with one of those big sandwich placards hangin' on her, listin' her phone number and all the lines of products that she sells. She also had these strong wires shootin' out from the top of the placard with an assortment of items from all her business lines danglin' on the very ends. There were assortments of Avon lipstick tubes, Mary Kay containers of blush, Tupperware bowls, Shaklee vitamins, and even bottles of Amway cleaners all suspended around Connie's head and shoulders. It really was cute, and she looked great. And she was right behind Nellie Tinkle, who was ridin' on her Tall Organs of the World float sponsored by her organ-tunin' company, Nellie's Tinklin' Organs. And just behind her was the Taco Tackle truck with this year's Miss Refried Beans, Little Linda. She won the title by bein' able to eat more refried beans than any of the other contestants durin' the annual December contest. Momma came in second, and Daddy said she bragged about it all night long if you catch my drift. Anyways, the whole parade was goin' just fine. Then for some reason or another that ain't quite clear, Wendy Bottom, who was drivin' the organ float, got the notion to slam on the brakes. Well, unknown to Connie Kay as she waved to the crowd and threw out tester items to the adorin' children, the float just a few feet in front of her had come to a dead stop. You can't imagine the sound that Connie Kay's face made when it ran smack dab into the back of that death trap. She went from lockin' in freshness to the cold asphalt of the street in less then a second. And the worse part was that she was covered from head to toe with lipstick, blush, and cleanin' products. And the vitamins were scattered all over the place. The Tupperware was fine. When they'd finally got her up to her feet, that mangled placard looked like it'd been through a twister. Even though it was tragic and Connie didn't make it to the end of the parade route, she did get a place in the Pangburn history books as the first parade casualty in the city. Little Linda took second place in the history books on account of Hubert throwin' on his brakes so he didn't run over Connie on the ground. This of course threw all 330 pounds of Little Linda airborne off the back of the Taco Tackle Shack truck and onto the Pangburn High School Marching Band just as they began playin' their always stirrin' rendition of "Ding Dong Merrily on High." Some of them poor kids will never be able to drink out of a bottle again, let alone suck on a straw.

Mickey Ray's momma, Wanda Kay, age sixty-five, lost her job as the Schwan's driver. That was really weird and eerie (see Lot #17). And as foretold to her, she did go open her own business. Every weekend she works her booth at the Flea Bath Flea Market over by Heber Springs, which she sure seems to enjoy. I'm sure you've seen other folks do the same kind of work that Wanda does. She puts you in front of a lovely background, takes your picture, and puts it on items that you've selected. The only thing is that her pictures are absolutely terrible. I swear I've never seen anythin' like it before in my life. She could take a picture of darkness and still have it overexposed. Everybody either looks like a ghost, one of her fingers is in the picture, or you're way off center. And I don't know how in the heck she does it. But of course, Wanda is so well loved that no one is willin' to say anythin', fearin' that they might hurt her feelin's. After all, she does so love this new job venture of hers. One day when we me, Momma, and Donna Sue was lookin' around at the Flea, purposely avoidin' the side of the buildin' where her booth is, she sneaked up behind us and said that we just had to come over and get our photos done. God bless her, she was so insistent and such a dear that, well, we couldn't help but go with her. She set us up in front of her digital camera that was up on this stationary tripod with its lens aimin' right at us. She counted to three and *flash*. Me, Momma, and Donna Sue each have a $12.95 high-quality dirt-resistant calendar for the year 2003 tucked away in a storage closet in each of our trailers bearin' a lovely vivid high-definition color photo of my right ear.

LOT #14

As most of y'all will recall from my holiday cookbook, I mentioned how Dottie and Opal Lamb's department store had burnt to the ground, but how luckily at that time all the items includin' the cash registers and store records had been moved to their newly built warehouse. Well, let me update you on what's been goin' on.

As you can easily guess, the old brick buildin' that had housed Lamb Department Store since 1927 was no more. The heat had been so intense that even the brick walls tumbled. But not bein' one to let life get her down, that next morinin' Dottie decided to just open the new warehouse up for the time bein' so folks could still buy what they needed. She's always been that way, thinkin' about the needs of others before she thinks about herself. Anyways, accordin' to both Dottie and her daughter, Opal, business hasn't been better since they've been runnin' the store out of the gigantic one-story warehouse. Why, they've even changed the company name. With the newly added bakery, one-hour photo counter, Daddy Lamb's Delivery Pizza booth, and beauty shop back over in the corner, the new Lamb's Super Store is sure to give any one of them big-time chains stores that might have thought about comin' to these parts a run for their money.

As for the old Lamb's location, well, Dottie used some of the insurance money to clear away the rubble and put up a bottlin' plant for her new line of soft drinks. Thanks to Lamb's Choice Sodas, the employment rate in the surrounding fifteen miles has dropped to zero. With flavors such as Lamb's Cola, Spite, Dr. Zipper, Mountain Don't, Orange Squash, and Schweatz's Ginger Ale, I'm sure that rate will remain low for years to come. As a matter of fact, Dottie says that she's havin' the hardest time findin' folks to fill the openin's she's got at Lamb's Super Store. I told her I'd put a plug in for her. So if you are a licensed beautician that knows how to work a doughnut-makin' machine and has a dependable car with enough room in the trunk for five large pizza boxes, please contact Dottie Lamb. Knowin' the difference between 100- and 200-speed film is a bonus.

Now Ben Beaver who, at age seventy, is still livin' with Dottie, has managed to continue runnin' Beaver Liquors and Wine as well as manage the High Chaparral Trailer Park for his daughter. But before you ask if that's just too much for a recently widowed fella in a wheelchair to handle, let me add that he has just hired on Harry and Elroy, who are now livin' in Lot #19 to help out part-time around Beaver Liquors. And he got Pastor Ida May Bee's husband, Brother Woody Bee, from Lot #7 to assist him with the keepin' up of the trailer park when Brother Woody ain't drivin' Pastor Ida May around town. Talk around the town is that he might even open a scaled-down version of Beaver Liquors in Lamb's Super Store. Of course, he'll have to find someone else to run it.

LOT #15

You know, when it comes to nice men, I don't think you could find any nicer ones than Kenny and Donny without goin' to the twelve Apostles first. And you should see their trailer. Every time I call on 'em, it's always immaculate and arranged so beautifully. It's just amazin' what these boys can do with plastic flowers. Anyways, since we last talked, Pastor Ida May Bee had just moved in, and I'd forgot to mention how well the Bees and Kenny and Donny had hit it off. They live right across from each other, so when the boys saw her and her husband, Brother Woody Bee, movin' their stuff into Lot #7, they went runnin' over and gave 'em a much-needed hand. Of course, I'd have jumped right in there and helped as well, but it was Saturday and *EastEnders* was on my BBCAmerica channel. Well, I guess that after all that movin', they all became best of friends and have spent a lot of time together over meals. So anyways, come last December when Pastor Ida May Bee was plannin' out the holiday events for the church, she contacted Kenny and Donny and asked if they'd put together the annual semi-live Nativity scene, which our church does every year. Of course the boys were surprised on account of 'em not bein' Baptist and all, but they were also honored and accepted the invitation. Now, I got to tell you folks that this job ain't an easy one, and I certainly wouldn't have wanted it, but when it was done, they'd kicked some butt.

The first thing they did was to move it from its traditional location outside of the church, and over to the Dusty Comet Auto Park Drive-In. Even though for the past eight years both our church, then headed by now former Pastor Hickey, and the drive-in have jointly been conductin' the yearly sold-out Christmas Eve service, which consists of a stirrin' sermon on the true meanin' of Christmas, an altar call, several offerin's thrown in here and there, and the showin' of Bruce Lee's *Fist of Fury*, this past December marked the first time the semi-live Nativity scene had made its home down by the playground in front of the gigantic screen. Not only were we able to charge a small $1-per-car fee for those who drove through to view the Nativity, but the walls helped to prevent any terrible incidents like the one we had the year before when a pack of wild dogs ran off with the baby Jesus, who was bein' played by the then Pastor Hickey's son, little Dick Hickey. Of course he was fine. Thanks to that unique musky stench that child gives off, the dogs spit him out just a half a block away. With the Hickeys no longer in town, there was great debate on who should play the Christ child. This debate was soon ended when we found out that one of the cliff divers that the Bunches use at the Taco Tackle Shack (see Lot #3) was a Baptist. Unfortunately for us, it happened to be the hairy one, but still, he was able to fit in the crib. Of course Sister Bertha played the part of Mary, and with a simple bedsheet placed just right, the wooden cigar Indian they got out front of the Gas and Smokes convenience store made the perfect Joseph. Listen, we was lucky to get the Indian, since no man wanted to set in one place for that long with Sister Bertha. Plus the wooden cigars carved into the Indian's hand simply made him look like he was passin' 'em out in celebration of his baby's birth. It fit right into the story line. The only problem we had was with the ass that Mary rode in on, which was masterfully played by my sister, Donna Sue. If Mary's real ass had been as drunk and confused as my sister was when she'd show up for the Nativity scene, our savior would've been born in Chickasha, Oklahoma. I tell you, my sister couldn't hardly see on some of them nights, let alone walk. And snore! Oh I tell y'all, it was bad. She'd make a bed out of the hay that was scattered around for effects and fall off to sleep. Her snorin' was so loud, Kenny had to crank up the Christmas music in an attempt to mask what sounded like the cries of a water buffalo in heat. Why, Sheriff Gentry said he was gettin' complaints from as far over as Searcy.

The costumes were just somethin' as well. Who would've thought to use feather boas and liquid beaded material on the wise men? And you'd be amazed at how AB stones placed just right on angel wings will bring out an angelic quality. Oh, and I can't even begin to tell you how many yards of taffeta must have gone into those shepherds' costumes. It sure was somethin' all right.

The boys did a great job, and if you overlooked the snorin' and the fact that our baby Jesus had a full beard and smoked Newport Slim 120s, it was really touchin', stirrin', and somethin' to behold.

LOT #16

For a while there my sister, Donna Sue, and my mother in-law, Momma Ballzak, weren't speakin'. It seemed that Donna Sue was madder than all get out when she heard that her High Chaparral drinkin' buddy had gone to work for her arch rival's daughter, Tina Faye Stopenblotter. Momma Ballzak knew that Donna Sue couldn't stand Faye Faye LaRue, and that she'd be bitter about the whole thing—but Momma Ballzak had no choice. You see, even though Momma Ballzak has been doin' a boomin' business sellin' her "trailer park Tupperware" and workin' her few hours a day on the cash register at the Pangburn Diner, she still was needin' an-other part-time job. Accordin' to Momma Ballzak, she couldn't buy what she used to with the amount of money she made, thanks to that newly in-creased sin tax that they just imposed in this part of the state. So when Tina Faye asked if she'd be interested in the house-keepin' position at her motel, she jumped on it. She comes in every day between 1:00 and 2:30 in the afternoon after gettin' off work at the Pangburn Diner and takes care of the rooms. Of course at first me and my husband, Dew, were afraid that takin' on another job at her age might be too much for Momma Ballzak, but when we found out that all she has to do each day is go into all the rooms and make the beds, and once a week change the towels and sheets, and give the bathtub and toilet a cleanin', we were just fine with her new employment. Plus it means that she's got less time to get into trouble. Eventually, after a drunken shoutin' match one Sunday afternoon outside her trailer home, she and Donna Sue finally made up after Momma Ballzak agreed to put food under the beds to draw roaches, and to leave a few books of matches from the Blue Whale Strip Club in each room.

LOT #17

Ain't it funny how you think you get to know somebody and then they up and shock you? That's the case with Faye Faye LaRue. As y'all might recall, she and my sister, Donna Sue, are rivals in the stripper world, and even though she caused my sister some heartache in the past, as far as I'm con-cerned that was thirty years or so ago. And like I always say, there comes a time when you just got to forgive and forget. Unless of course they did somethin' to you, and in that case you might as well forget that whole for-givin' thing, 'cause I'll go to my grave cursin' your doggone name. Any-ways, since Faye Faye moved back into the High Chaparral, she's always been nice to me, and I'm always cordial back unless my sister happens to be nearby, and I think Faye Faye understands that I can't say nothin' to her in those cases. But since Donna Sue is either sleepin' all day long or out at her pawnshop, I get to talk a lot to Faye Faye. And just as is the case with my sister, I even see her with her daughter at church from time to time. But I've thought Faye Faye was a nice person for a slut, and as I've got to know her better, I've really enjoyed her wit and quick tongue, and I mean that in the nicest way possible. Well anyways, I find out that this woman who I thought was rather simple compared to other strippers that I've known over the years, has actually been hidin' a special talent. It seems that our own Ms. Faye Faye LaRue has psychic abilities. That's right, dear reader, Faye Faye is the Kenny Kingston of the High Chaparral Trailer Park.

Wanda was the first to discover Faye Faye's hidden talents when, one day while gasin' up the truck at the Gas and Smokes Convenience Store, Faye Faye walked up to her and said that after she dropped off the truck to go home and stay in bed the next day, and not to take any calls from her work. Well, she might have wondered why, but that's what Wanda did. Later that day Faye Faye stopped by and told her that the people at work were out to get her and it would be best to stay home another day, and to avoid usin' the phone. So again Wanda followed what Faye Faye had told her, and amazingly enough her work did call the trailer. Faye Faye warned Wanda that since her work was out to get her she should stay at home for a total of four days. And on that fifth day when Wanda did go back to work, you will never believe what happened to her. They fired her! Can you believe that? Faye Faye was right on the money with her predictions. Oh, I get chills just thinkin' about it. Anyways, Faye Faye told Wanda not worry, she would be startin' her own business soon, and it would be doin' somethin' that she liked. Notice that Faye Faye never said it would be somethin' Wanda was good at. Let me just make sure that we're all clear on that point. Wanda couldn't wait to tell all of us what'd happened to her, and before you knew it, people were settin' up appointments to have Faye Faye give 'em a readin'. Even though I ain't into all that stuff, I still think it's fun, and from what I can tell, Faye Faye is pretty good at what she does. I'm tryin' to talk her into doin' a trailer park horoscope book. Wouldn't that be somethin' now?

Speakin' of shockin' news, Faye Faye's daughter, Tina Faye Stopenblotter (she's thirty now, my Lord), has certainly had a lot goin' on since we last spoke. It took a death to finally reveal who her real father was. You see, Faye Faye had never come out with that information even to her own daughter. But when a detective from Little Rock came to Lot #17 with a $100,000 inheritance check made out to Tina Faye, the cat finally came out of the bag. Come to find out, Tina Faye was the illegitimate daughter of the recently deceased 103-year-old right honorable state senator Raymond Ulysses Watts. R.U., which was what he preferred to be called, had been a bigwig in the state senate as well as the Democratic Party. He finally retired just three years back on account of health. Of course he served his last two terms from his office laid up in a hospital bed. But R.U. did a lot for both the state as well as the fine people of Arkansas durin' his seventy-three years in office. He always kept an eye out for the seniors in his district as well to make sure that they got a fair shake

Well, Tina Faye took that money and bought a little piece of land down by the highway where she built a small thirteen-room motel. Despite her mother's disapproval, she named her new business in honor of her late daddy. Just this past March the R.U. Inn opened for business. And in the tradition of her daddy, Tina offers a special nightly rate of $9 for all seniors sixty years or older. And to make sure that travelin' elderly know about this deal, Tina has put up a big sign that can be seen from the highway. So regardless of which way you're drivin' you can clearly read the billboard, which invites all motorists to stop in at the R.U. INN FOR A SIXTY-NINER.

LOT #18

When it comes to me and my husband, Dew, y'all pretty much already know what's goin' on in our lives, thanks to the ever-present media that follows me around like a pack of jocks on a cheerleader. I do have to admit that I enjoy their attention, as well as yours. All the kind gifts, money orders, personal checks, and cash that you send me by way of my publisher let me know just how much you, my lovely fans, care about me. Of course I'm also thrilled each time y'all sign on to my Web pages at www.rubyann. org and take the time to sign my guest book or simply send me an e-mail. And even though I do appreciate the time you spend attachin' and downloadin' those nude photos of yourself to your e-mail, it really ain't necessary, and in most cases, it's just revoltin'. And as y'all know, if you ever wonder where I'm gonna be or when I'll appear on TV next, you can always go to my Web pages to find out.

I know that there are lots of irons in the fire, as the old sayin' goes, when it comes to projects that I'm workin' on. And if things work out, you never know, I might just end up bein' the spokesperson for IHOP or the new catalog model for Big Lots! Just keep your fingers crossed and your prayers comin'. I'll keep you posted.

As for my husband, Dew, he's just fishin'. He hates the spotlight, so he pretty much stays around Lot #18 when I'm out on the road these days. He does keep real busy with his hobbies. He just loves to go out by the lake and fish. He has been tryin' somethin' new. He calls it Ruby Ann trollin'. What he does is he takes a couple of my old bras and ties a little weight to each one. Then he gets a buddy of his to start up the outboard motor and as they drive around the lake, my husband, Dew, drops my bras in the water. The weights pull 'em down toward the bottom, and then all he does is pull 'em back up while the boat is movin'. Why, the first time he and his buddy gave it a try, they caught close to sixty trout just in the first hour. Of course they let 'em all go, but they sure had a good time. My husband, Dew, says the fish seem to have a lot less fight in 'em when you pull 'em into the boat. He thinks it's on account of 'em gettin' all tuckered out from tryin' to escape by swimmin' the length of my speedin' brassiere. I think he's jokin'.

LOT #19

After the death of her beloved husband, Jimmy Janssen, we all knew it'd just be a matter of time before Jeannie moved off to live with one of her preacher boys. And sure enough both Jack and Josh came up right before Thanksgivin' and carted her and all her belongin's away. She'll split the year livin' between their homes in Mississippi and Louisiana. We sure hated to see dear sweet Jeannie leave, but that garage sale they had was one humdinger.

It didn't take any time for the Janssen twins to find someone to take over the lease at Lot #19. And since they threw in the forty-year-old trailer along with the lot, there were lots of folks jumpin' at the chance to get their hands on it. But after the big controversy that took place when Faye

Faye LaRue and her daughter, Tina Faye, moved in last year, Ben Beaver wisely decided to form a residence board, which would have to approve anyone before they could lease a lot at the High Chaparral Trailer Park. Bein' the bigwig that I am, I of course held a seat on that said board along with Nellie Tinkle of Lot #4, Sister Bertha of Lot #12, and Momma Ballzak of Lot #16. Seein' how this was our first actual board meetin', we weren't sure of what to expect. Ben Beaver, who held the fifth seat of the five-member commission, ran the closed-door meetin' and presented the names of the twelve people who'd said they was interested in movin' into our fine community. Now, it wouldn't be right for me to list all those names, so I'll just tell you who we selected and why. It was a unanimous decision to give the green light to town mortician Vance Pool. I voted for Vance 'cause he used to date my sister and I wanted his sorry behind to have to look her in the eye every day of the week so he could see what he missed out on (of course he sees her every Monday night when they work together at the Blue Whale or once every two weeks when, for a six-pack of cold beer, she goes down to the funeral home and lays naked on a slab so he can practice his mortician makeup skills on her face). Sister Bertha gave him the go so that she could keep an eye on him (400-pound Vance Pool moonlights at the Blue Whale on Monday night under the name of Vance Poole the American Tenderloin, exotic dancer extraordinaire). Nellie Tinkle gave him the thumbs-up 'cause he's been a close personal friend of her family for years. Ben voted in favor of Vance on account of the wonderful job he did on Ben's late wife Dora, and Momma Ballzak welcomed him into the park in hopes that he'd do a wonderful job on her when the time came. Of course we did include a stipulation that he couldn't bring any dead bodies into the trailer park. After all, that's my sister, Donna Sue's job.

Within a day, after Jeannie had moved out, Vance Pool (he's a bit over forty, but not much) had moved all his stuff in. Now, seein' how the trailer was a two-bedroom, Vance invited his two fellow male dancers Harry Lombardi, age sixty-four, and Elroy Dasafe, age eighty, who together make up the dancin' troop Vance Pool and His Beef Stick Boys, to move in with him. And as anyone who knows Elroy will tell you, wherever he goes, his dog, Zero, goes. Now I don't know what kind of dog Zero is, but I can sure tell you that he's old. God bless him, he's got to be goin' on twenty-seven by now. The vet in town says he's never seen a dog live to be that old before. He's in good shape except for the fact that Elroy has to hold his leg up for him when he pees. Other than that, he's just fine. Well anyways, gettin' back to the story, Harry and Elroy decided to just use the Janssen twin's old bunk beds, which Jeannie had left. Since Harry is terrified of heights, Elroy took the top bunk. Of course he wasn't able to climb the ladder up to the top bunk. He just rode his adjustable chair, which he kept by the side of the bed, all the way up the top and then simply climbed over. It was the perfect situation, or so they had thought. What no one had taken into consideration was the fact that Zero had bladder control problems and every night as he slept curled up with Elroy, he'd pee the bed. It didn't bother Elroy 'cause he did too from time to time, which came as a big surprise to sleepin' Harry down below. Of course, since Harry couldn't sleep up on the top bunk, it meant that some other kind of sleepin' arrangements would have to be made. As luck would have it, a large shed that Jimmy Jensen had used for a little wood shop (he loved Tool Time), had come along with the property. Well before you could say "Singing in the Rain" Harry had helped Elroy clean the shed up and turned it into a small bedroom where Elroy and Zero could urinate the night away in peace. Vance had come up with the idea of runnin' the hose from the dryer out into the shed durin' the winter months so Elroy had heat durin' the night. With the exception of the enormous lint balls that build up from time to time, the place is wonderful. Of course, Vance and Harry have to get up in the middle of the night when that dryer buzzer goes off so they can restart it, or poor Elroy and Zero could freeze to death. Needless to say, Vance and Harry are shoppin' around for a new dryer with a longer dry cycle.

LOT #20

If y'all take a minute to think back, y'all will recall that I mentioned in my last book that Lovie Birch had been spendin' a lot of time talkin' with both state and national leaders in the Democratic Party, which both her and her husband, Elmer, have been real bigwigs in at the local level. Well, I just got word that by the time this book hits the stores, there'll be a for-sale sign in the window of their newspaper the *Pangburn Bugle*, and both Lovie and Elmer will be hitchin' up their trailer and relocatin' it to the Flaming Flamingo Trailer Park in beautiful Miami, Florida. That's right, dear reader, you've heard it here first. The Democratic Party, which all of us at the High Chaparral belong to, has decided that they need folks like Lovie and Elmer to be in Florida durin' the November elections. Nobody wants to risk the same kind of votin' scandal that took place in that gorgeous state durin' the last two elections. And trust me when I say if anybody can make sure that things go right, it's Lovie. I've never known a gal that was as organized as she is. Not only did she never mess up my Avon order, which I wish I could say now that Connie Kay has taken it over, but she was able to throw a Tupperware party in her bedroom while at the same time host-ess a state Democratic fund-raiser in her livin' room. That was surely some-thin' to behold.

As far as their newspaper goes, I don't know what's gonna happen to it. I can guarantee you the new owner won't be nothin' but a card-carryin' Democrat. Rumor has it that when the Birches leaked out the news that the *Bugle* might be up for grabs, some out-of-town folks showed interest, as did Sister Bertha. Well, y'all can trust me when I say that I'll buy the paper myself before I'll see Sister Bertha's hands on it. Both Lovie and Elmer did ask me if I'd be interested in buyin' the *Bugle* since they knew I was a good old dyed-in-the-wool Democrat, but I just don't think I'm cut out to be the new Katharine Graham. I just have to see how it goes. I know that Dottie Lamb might want to buy the *Bugle*, but I'm sure if she does, we can count on seein' large pictures of her godforsaken daughter smeared all over each issue. Oh, that's enough to make me take out my checkbook and write the Birches a hot check right this minute.

Goodbye, Lovie and Elmer. We folks at the High Chaparral Trailer Park will miss you, and Lot #20 will never be the same. By the way, we don't know who exactly is movin' in to their vacant lot yet, but I'll keep you posted.

Ruby Ann's
Down Home Trailer Park
BBQin' Cookbook

Chapter 1

Here is my sister, Donna Sue, BBQin' up a steak outside her trailer. I told the old cow that with the money she makes workin' down at the Blue Whale Strip Club she ought to go out and get her a new BBQ. But, oh no, she thinks that little hibachi she bought off an old boyfriend for $237 is good enough. Of course it took her two and a half hours to cook this dang steak.

How to Select Your BBQ Grill

In the old days it used to be easy to BBQ without much thought on what kind of grill to use. Of course that was on account of the fact that we trailer park folks didn't really have lots of choices back then. You could either get a store-bought one, which was pretty much out of the question for my kind, or you could make your own. The first grill I can remember my folks usin' was one they'd put together from rocks, charcoal, and metal coat hangers that had been bound together with wire. Of course then there was Ollie White and her late husband, Orville, over in Lot #10 who use to tilt one of their metal outside chairs over the coals and use the grated back as their cookin' surface. And I can't begin to tell you how many great pieces of meat I had when neighbors Nellie and C. M. Tinkle in Lot #4 would from time to time take the grill off their 1931 Chevy four-door sedan and throw a neighborhood BBQ. Regardless of what selection of beef they'd cook up, it all had that wonderful flavor of hickory wood and Prestone. Even today, the smell of an overheated Chevy gets my taste buds excited.

Nowadays, when you can pick up a cheap little hibachi or even a tiny tabletop gas grill for under $20, there ain't no real reason why a person in the trailer park can't own a store-bought unit. But let me tell y'all, buyin' a BBQ can be a pain in the neck. You got more cookers out there on the market than Santa Fe has adobe huts! Even Wal-Mart carries at least three or four different types of BBQs. So what is a person to do? Well, you're in luck. I've gone out and done all the homework for y'all. Yes, I've taken the time to cook on and eat cookin' from almost every type of grill known to man or woman, just so you don't have to. I've also come to a conclusion about which company is the best and would gladly be their spokesperson if they'd only ask (of course a small fee and a brand-new top-of-the-line grill with all them fancified extras would be nice to have as well). But for now, dear reader, I'm gonna do my best to help turn this confusin' chore into an effortless task that's almost as easy as my sister and as simple as my niece. I'm gonna lay all the facts out on the table about each kind of BBQer that there is on the market today and let you choose which one is right for you. This will eliminate any kind of misunderstandin' that you could possibly have and will make your shoppin' experience so trouble free and thoughtless that even my dear old senile Me-Ma could select a BBQer and not go wrong. With that said, let's take a gander at what we got to pick from.

THE HIBACHI

As you read earlier, the hibachi was what my sister had at one time. Now, the good thing about one of these is that they are small and portable, so they can be stored anywhere. The bad thing is that they are small and portable, so you can't cook lots of food at one time. I know that when my sister would make dinner for her and a date on the BBQ, she'd have to cook two burgers, then two more burgers, then grill the buns, and finally BBQ the corn. With the time it took to get that thing hot, she'd spend almost an hour and a half to two hours just to make a simple four-burger meal with a vegetable. But if you live in an apartment or small trailer or you ain't got much of a yard, this thing is great. And I even saw one on the market that folded out to form a larger grillin' area but was still portable and took up no space at all when it came to storin' it. It was called the Son of Hibachi and I think you can get it on the Web. Just tell 'em Ruby Ann Boxcar sent you.

So if you're lookin' for somethin' to use at tailgate parties, on the beach, or in your trunk while drivin' across the U.S., this is perfect for you. Also if you're a single person and you'd never want to cook anythin' other than a few hamburgers or a small steak, go out an get yourself one of these.

THE BRAIZER

When Momma and Daddy finally did go out and buy a real-life BBQ it was a brazier. It had four legs that resembled the legs on a TV tray, and you'd snap your top part onto these legs. Some models have the traditional three legs, and some are even on wheels. These were real big in the fifties. You put your coals in the firebox, which is about four to six inches deep, and then lay the grill on top of these metal things that come straight up out of it. You can raise the grill from the heat by simply pickin' up the grill and puttin' it on the next notch of them metal things. Once these things cool down, and as long as the legs easily come off, this BBQ is pretty easy to tuck away as well. The downfall is that most models don't have lids, there ain't no vents to control the air, and you got to scoop out the ashes when you're done. Another model of this is a tabletop version, which is very small, so it's also easy to store in small places.

THE KETTLE

I heard somebody say that these are one of the most popular non-gas BBQs on the market today, and I can see why. With a kettle's deep firebox, it's easy to BBQ or even smoke large pieces of meat. It also means that you got a better chance of cookin' out in the wind than you do with the other BBQ grills I've mentioned so far. There are vents so you can regulate the airflow and even a hole in the bottom for the ashes. Kettles are great for families who love to BBQ. The only downfall in my mind is that after an hour or so you got to really work to keep the cookin' temperatures at one level.

After Pa-Pa passed away, my Me-Ma refused to use hers, sayin' it was just to darn big for her. So instead, on Halloween, she'd pull it out of the storage shed she had next to her trailer and park it next to the cinder block steps in front of her door. Then she'd fill that whole big bottom kettle part with candy. This way when the kids came around trick or treatin' they could take the candy out of it rather than ringin' her doorbell and upsettin' her dog, Floppy. This was a treat for all the kids and went on until the year we took her to the home. That year she set it up in front of her trailer, but with the way her mind was goin' she filled it up with charcoal and lit it. Needless to say, many kids were surprised that year, but she did make it up the next day by goin' from trailer to trailer passin' out grilled carrots and raw potato pieces wrapped in cabbage. Oh, you can just imagine how happy the kids were then!

THE GAS GRILL

If you got the space for one of these babies, then I'd have to suggest your lookin' into gettin' one of 'em. Not only does it take just five to ten minutes to get it up to the point that you're ready to cook, but you also ain't got the mess of those doggone coals. And there is no ash to take care of for the most part. It's easy to light regardless of what time of year it might be, and since you can maintain a steady temperature for long periods of time, you can easily cook indirectly on this thing as well. The only downfall on this is the large size, but the upswing on it is that 'cause of its size, you can actually BBQ large pieces of meat or big meals for large gatherin's. And you can find a gas grill that will fit most of your budgets. And if you was wonderin', this is what all of us at the High Chaparral use, includin' my sister, who has to get state approval before she can even turn the knob on the propane handle.

THE SMOKER

This is real nice if you're just gonna be smokin' all your food. Personally I don't like 'em, 'cause you can't grill a burger or a steak on these things, but if you already have a grill for that, then this would be a great accent tool to have.

THE KITCHEN GRILL

I'm sure y'all have seen these in some of the fancier trailers or in trailers whose kitchens have been remodeled. These typically are gas or electric and they got grates on the top. They're real handy if you want BBQ but you don't want to go outside. Since these are part of the stove, they can cost a pretty penny, and unless you just need a new stove, they ain't for you.

Well, there you go. I hope this has helped you make a decision on what kind of BBQ to buy. Just remember three things: don't get somethin' that you won't use; don't get somethin' that's too small; and when you do get a BBQ, don't even think about usin' it until you've read Chapter 2. Enough said for now.

Chapter 2

When it comes to BBQin', old Jack Frost don't bother us trailer folks. For that matter, if he'll bring a covered dish that ain't got ambrosia salad in it, why, I'll be Baptist enough to slap him on a burger or two—just as soon as I'm sure there's enough BBQ for me.

BBQin' Basics

COMMON BBQIN' TERMS

Before we even think about strikin' a match or turnin' on the gas, we need to make sure we understand all the highfalutin words that BBQers like to throw around when they get to talkin' about the fine art of top-of-the-line cookin'. This is important for two reasons. You don't want to look like a complete fool in front of your family, even though they might already think you are, and you don't want to burn your trailer down just because you didn't understand what was bein' told to you.

An example of the dangers that one can experience by simply not understandin' the lingo would be the time I told dear old Ollie White of Lot #10 that she could get her charcoals burnin' a lot faster if she'd simply light some crumpled-up papers in her chimney starter. Well, God bless her, she literally took me at my word and lit some crumpled-up newspapers in her trailer's chimney. Now, typically that would be somethin' that everyone would get a laugh from with no harm done. But in a trailer, there ain't no built-in chimneys, but rather just those fake plastic or cardboard ones, which happened to be the kind I'm talkin' about in this case. Well, by the time Ollie realized somethin' was terribly wrong, that fire she started had grown to be too much for a little old in-home fire extinguisher to handle, so she came out of her trailer yellin' bloody murder. Luckily my husband, Dew, was outside practicin' his fishin' pole castin' when Ollie started yellin'. Dew was able to drag out the blazin' cardboard fireplace, but Ollie's wall and part of the carpet was burnin' like crazy by then. And on account of it bein' a Sunday and the volunteer fire department off for the Lord's day, we had to quickly hook the pickup tuck of our neighbor over in Lot #3, Hubert Bunch, to the trailer and have him race it over to the boat docks on the lake. Luckily Hubert was able to back Ollie's mobile home into the lake and put out the fire before it could do much more damage. Not only was Ollie's trailer saved, but, thanks to an open window and a torn screen, when they parked her trailer back on Lot #10, Ollie discovered that she'd managed to catch six trout, two catfish, and a boot.

So make sure you read and go over each term that follows. It's important that you know each one like the back of your hand. And if you have any doubts about the significance of knowin' these words, just take a look behind that large velvet Elvis tapestry with the lighted twinklin' eyes for a 3-D effect that Ollie's got hangin' on her wall. Enough said, I think.

Bastin': This here is when you brush on a sauce, glaze, marinade, oil, or liquid of some kind while your meat is cookin' to make sure it stays moist and flavorable.

Bastin' brush: Typically this is a long-handled brush that you use when you baste.

Briquettes: These horse-poop-shaped lumps are basically ground charcoal and coal dust that've been pressed and compacted together to create a heatin' unit when lighted.

Brochette: This is simply a fancified way of sayin' kabob. Faye Faye LaRue likes to throw this term around a lot with her kabob recipes. I think she picked it up the term when she lived in New Orleans or some place like that where they use them French terms a lot. Needless to say, it just ticks my sister off every time Faye Faye uses it. "If she's too good to say kabob like every other proud American," says my sister, Donna Sue, "then maybe she should pack her trailer up and go over to France to live."

Broilin': This is a type of cookin' where the heat source is right under or directly over the food item like a steak or burger. This locks or seals in the flavor and juices.

BTU: Now this stands for British Thermal Unit, and it's just a way of measurin' how hot a gas grill can get. Don't worry if your grill ain't got a high BTU ratin', 'cause it ain't got nothin' to do with your BBQs cookin' muscle. With that said, you will need at least a 25,000-BTU ratin' on your grill if you want to be able to cook most of the items in this here book.

Buns: Normally these are the bread kind that you serve your hamburgers or wienies on. But you'll also want to keep an eye on where your own personal buns are at all times so as not to burn 'em accidentally on the BBQ grill.

Ceramic briquettes: You'll find these instead of charcoal briquettes in gas grills. Unlike the briquettes made from charcoal, these ceramic cousins don't burn up completely. In some gas grills you'll have lava rocks or metal plates that work just like these ceramic briquettes. When the drippin's from the food you're BBQin' hit these babies, they put off a smoke that flavors what you're cookin'.

Charcoal: These little black horse-poop-shaped lumps are simply wood that's had the gases and moisture burnt clean out of it.

Charcoal grate: This is the holder where you put your charcoal or briquettes.

Charcoal grill: This is one of them grills that uses some form of charcoal for its main fuel or heat source.

Chimney starter: This kind of starter is a metal cylinder with a handle on it that lets you hold hot coals for starting a fire.

Direct grillin': This type of grillin' is a fast way of cookin' your food where the item is placed directly over the heat source.

Drip pan: This is the container that catches all your juices that drip off the meat when you cook it.

Dry smokin': This is a type of cookin' where you put your food item directly over the heat, close the lid, and allow the smoke from the drippin's and all to cook and flavor the food. Typically this is used with charcoal to add a woodsy taste, but it can be done with gas grills as well.

Electric charcoal lighter: Now, this little puppy is handy if you want to light your charcoal without the use of lighter fluid. The only problem with it is that it requires an outlet in order to use it.

Firebox: The main part of the grill where the heatin' area is located on both charcoal grills and gas grills is called the firebox.

Flare-ups: This is when your flame rises up on account of drippin's hittin' the briquettes, lava rocks, or charcoal lumps.

Gas grill: This is a grill that uses gas as its main heatin' source to cook food.

Glaze: This is a shiny coatin' you put on food as it cooks, usually by basting it.

Grill basket: This is two thin wire grills that are hinged together so you can put your less-easy-to-flip food items like fish or sandwiches inside. When you need to flip the food item, you just turn the grill basket over. It's real easy to use.

Grill rack: This is the grate or grid where your food sets while it BBQs.

Grill wok: This utensil is great for stir-fry.

Indirect grillin': This is a way of slow cookin' your food so it cooks evenly. You got your heat source away from the food item so it can BBQ at a low temperature. This method requires that you keep your BBQ lid on for most the cookin' time. It is also great for large cuts of meat as well as breads and desserts.

Kabobs: These are made with pieces of meat, veggies, and sometimes fruit that are placed on long pieces of metal or wood called skewers.

Lighter fluid: Be careful with this stuff 'cause it can give your food items the worst-tastin' flavor if you don't use it right. Just remember, you're only tryin' to light a few coals, not signal aliens on other planets.

Marinatin': When you let your meat set in a liquid mixture that you've made up, it helps to make the meat more tender and tasty. I always suggest that when you use a marinade you let your meats soak at least three hours before cookin'. Just remember to always marinate in the fridge and never out on a counter. The last thing you want is to get a hold of some bad meat. Just ask my sister.

Meat thermometer: Nowadays this little cook's helper is a must when BBQin'. You can get a cheap one or you can even get one that is digital. Just make sure that when you use it, you get it in the thickest part of the meat, away from any bones.

Medium doneness: The middle of your meat should be slightly red or pink. You will know you've reached this level of cookin' when the inside temperature of the meat is 160 degrees F.

Medium-rare doneness: The inside should be very pink or red in the center. When you get to a readin' of 145 degrees F., your meat is now medium rare.

Medium–well doneness: Just a hint of pink is what you want to find in a medium–well done piece of meat. The temperature should be around 165 degrees F.

Rare doneness: This is when the meat has been on the grill just long enough to sear it on both sides. The internal meat temperature is 130 to 135 degrees F.

Rotisserie: This is a long metal skewer that hangs over your heat source. Personally none of us at the High Chaparral ever use these things when we cook.

Rub: This is a set of spices or ingredients that you've combined and rubbed on the meat before you put it on the grill to BBQ.

Sauce: Now, there are two kinds of sauce. There is the kind that you use to baste your meat, and there is the kind that you serve with your meat after it's cooked. And both kinds of sauces can be one and the same. Just remember to never dip your bastin' brush or mop in a sauce and then serve that same bowl of sauce with the meat. If you do this accidentally, then go and boil that sauce before servin' it. There are many different recipes for sauces as well and we will get into all that later on.

Self-lightin' charcoal briquettes: Nothin' says, "MMM good" like coal that's been soaked in lighter fluid for days. Just remember that this might give your food a petroleum taste if they ain't used correctly.

Skewers: These are usually long metal or wooden sticks that you put food items on and then place on a grill. When usin' wooden skewers, you got to soak 'em in somethin' so they get nice and wet.

Smoker box: This is a box that you put your wood chips in and set on the charcoals or gas flame when you want to smoke your food. We can also use a homemade smoker bag that will do basically the same thing.

Tools: We'll get into these later on, but basically they are the items you need to BBQ.

Vents: These are holes that allow you to control the amount of air that comes into your firebox.

Well doneness: The whole thing inside and out should be a nice brown color, and the temperature should be 170 degrees F.

Wood chips and chunks: These give your food a smoky flavor as they burn on the coals or briquettes. Usually you soak 'em first so that they smoke for a while rather than just ignite and burn away.

WHEN TO BBQ

Regardless of the event or meal, anytime is a good time to BBQ. I know some folks out there are like, "Boy, Ruby Ann, with the cost of meat, BBQin' all the time is a bit out of my budget." And of course, to that I say, "Don't be an idiot, stupid." It don't matter what kind of food your makin', you can always add that special flavor and taste by simply BBQin' it rather than poppin' it into the oven or microwave. This may sound strange to some of y'all who think the only thing you can do on a BBQ is cook your meat, but I'm here to tell you that, given the time and the right kind of grill, nothin' is impossible. So trust me when I say that, thanks to this book, BBQin' ain't just about heatin' up your wienie no more.

There're some days that you'll certainly want to make sure and BBQ on. I'm talkin' about those special days like your birthday, anniversary, graduation from kindergarten (don't wait for the big one from high school, 'cause that day may never come), the day you was baptized, your first communion, bar or bas mitzvah, family reunions, funerals, when a close relative is on *Cops,* when that close relative gets out of jail, when that same said relative makes the FBI's most wanted list, after a sportin' event (notice I didn't mention winnin' anywhere in that portion at all), holidays, weekends, or even when you get a big job promotion (right, like that's gonna happen in that dead-end job you got). These days especially are meant for good times and great food. So call up your friends or neighbors, tell 'em to bring over some meat, and light up the old grill for a night to remember. And if you really want it to go down in history, include liquor. Yes, nothin' can turn a fun-filled evenin' into a real-life event more than cheap booze, good BBQ, and folks who make less than $6 an hour. Trust me on this one, 'cause after all I can see my sister's trailer lot from my front window.

WHEN NOT TO GRILL

All right, folks, let's nip this one right in the bud. There are some books out there that'll tell you that you shouldn't grill when it's cold outside or when it's rainin' or durin' a lightnin' storm. Well, these folks are obviously not livin' in a trailer park or even in the real world for that matter. I mean at the High Chaparral we cook year-round. I don't care if there're ten feet of snow on the ground, somebody's BBQin' somethin'! Why, I remember as a young girl watchin' Daddy go outside to flip burgers durin' a twister. Mind you, he wasn't stupid. He'd tied a good long rope between him and the fridge as well as weighed himself down with pocketfuls of loose change before headin' out where the front door had been just seconds before. Even though there were pieces of straw that had been driven right through 'em by the wind, those were some of the best-tastin' burgers I can remember. By the way, me and my husband have learned over the years that if you leave the air vents opened just right, the burgers will actually turn themselves durin' a twister.

Of course, if there's a lightnin' storm goin' on, you'll want to take precautions. For example, send someone else out to flip the burgers, with a plastic spatula of course. Or, park your car right next to the trailer door so you can jump in, drive over to the grill, roll your window down and flip the meat, and then drive back to the door. Everybody knows that you're safe from lightnin' when you're in a car (I don't know if this is true with anything other than Fords, General Motors, or Chryslers).

So, basically the question of when not to grill in a trailer park is like askin' when not to watch wrestlin'. If you get creative, there ain't never a reason not to fire up that BBQ. And just remember, dear reader, even with severe contractions, pregnant women can still physically drive a car by themselves.

TOOLS OF THE TRADE

Unless you're like the Bionic Man, and can pick up burnin' hot items without feelin' it, there are some tools that you're just goin' to have to break down and buy. Or you can be like some of the cheap folks who live around me and just improvise. Anyways, here is what you'll have to have before you start BBQin'.

By the way, before y'all start sendin' hateful e-mail to me at rubylot18@ aol.com (I love to read your e-mails and try to answer every one myself) sayin' that I forgot to add the turnin' fork to my list, let me just tell y'all here and now that I don't like those forks. I never do recommend addin' the forks to your tool list 'cause sure as you do, somebody is goin' to take that thing and poke your meat with it. As we all know now, on steaks, wienies, and basically any good meat, when you pierce it, all those great-tastin' juices flow right out and you end up with a dry piece of nothin'. So I suggest you take my advice and forget that item when you stock your BBQ tools.

Apron: This item is used to avoid gettin' grease, sauce, and other things on your clothes that might stain 'em.

    Substitute: Take an old dress and tie the cuffs of the sleeves together. Put this part over your head, and you got a stylish new apron.

Bastin' brush: This item is real handy when you need to baste small meats with BBQ sauce, extra marinade, or a rich buttery sauce while your food item is BBQin'. Its long handle helps to keep you away from the heat.

    Substitute: An old paintbrush that you use when doin' the trim is just about the right size for this job. Just clean it up real, real good and tie it to the end of a long stick and you're ready to commence with the bastin'.

Chimney starter: This is great if you use a charcoal grill. It's an elongated tube with a grate in one end. You stuff crumpled-up paper in it followed by charcoal. You light the paper and it in turn heats up the charcoal. This helps to get your coals ready for the grill. It also has a handle on the side so you can easily move it around or simply turn it over to empty the coals into the firebox.

    Substitute: Grab an old empty two-pound coffee can and take the bottom end off. Drive a few nails around the bottom and, goin' through from the top openin', stuff a little chicken wire in the can so it rests on them nails you done put in. When you get ready to use it, put your crumpled-up paper in the top of the can and onto the chicken wire, followed by your coals. A pair of long-handled pliers works great for movin' or tiltin' your brand-new homemade chimney starter.

Fire extinguisher: This is nice to have around just in case somethin' goes wrong and you start a fire. When it comes to BBQin', safety first is the number one rule.

    Substitute: Me-Ma with a garden hose.

Grill basket: You won't believe how great this little device is until you use it. You can put items in a grill basket, which looks like two small grills attached to each other, and easily turn 'em without worryin' about 'em fallin' through the cracks of the grill or just plain old fallin' apart.

    Substitute: Two old window screens or, for that matter, metal screen doors duct-taped together will just about do the same thing, even though they'll take up your entire cookin' space on the BBQ and more. Just make sure to keep the duct tape portions away from the fire. Cleanin' the screens before usin' 'em is optional.

Grill topper: This flat surface with small holes in it is great for cookin' fish and brownin' bread, or other items that might fall through the grill or burn quickly if direct fire hits 'em.

    Substitute: To save money, you can easily take a nail and hammer to an old cookie sheet, and get just about the same effect. Once again, you menfolk need to check with your other halves before drivin' lots of holes in that cookie sheet.

Grill wok: When you have to grill up some onions or other veggies or even brown crumbled hamburger meat, this is the best. It's shaped like a wok, but it's made to set right on top the grillin' area of your BBQ.

    Substitute: An old hubcap works great, just make sure it's metal or you'll have a mess that'll take you hours to clean up.

Heavy-duty oven mitts: Since your hands can easily get burnt when you're BBQin', these thicker-than-your-typical mitts are a must-have.

Nothin' can ruin a fun time around a BBQ more than an unnecessary burn. Of course a passin' bird poopin' on your steak pretty much puts a damper on a cookout as well, but that just comes with the territory. But wearin' a pair of heavy-duty oven mitts can prevent singed hands.

Substitute: Two of those thick motel bathroom floor towels wrapped around each hand work pretty good at keepin' the heat from your hands as well.

Kabob fork: You can actually put three kabobs on this one three-pronged fork. Who would have ever thought?

Substitute: A pitchfork works wonders and can easily be found in an old deserted barn or at your local junkyard.

Long-handled spatulas: One of these metal spatulas with long wooden handles allows you to turn what you're grillin' from a safe distance.

Substitute: A spatula duct-taped to the end of a yardstick does the same thing.

Long-handled tongs: These are a must for turnin' steaks, wienies, and all other kinds of meat that you might be BBQin'.

Substitute: Metal tongs with two-yard sticks duct-taped, one on each side, to 'em is easy to use with a little practice. Once again, keep an eye on the duct tape when you get close to fire.

Meat thermometer: It's important that you keep track of the temperature of your meat when cookin' it. You can do this by usin' a long meat thermometer. They even have some that are digital. This is a must for all BBQs.

Substitute: An old metal hog rectal thermometer from back when I was just a little girl raisin' a hog every year works just fine.

Sauce mop: You use this device when you're moppin' on your BBQ sauce, extra marinade, glaze, or any other kind of bastin' solution that you might want to apply to a large food item while it BBQs. Usually these have a handle that's about eighteen inches long, so you don't burn yourself while usin' it.

Substitute: An old mop with its handle cut down a bit works just great. Men, make sure before you cut on that handle that what you got is your wife's old mop and not her good one. The last thing you want to do is BBQ with a broken arm and a concussion.

Sauce spray bottle: Instead of bastin', when your sauce is thin enough you can simply pour it into one of these bottles and spray it on the meat from time to time as it BBQs.

Substitute: A cleaned-out Windex bottle works great as well for this job. Yes, you must clean it out first unless you want your burger to taste streak free.

Skewers: You can get either metal skewers or wooden skewers, which must be soaked in water before you use 'em. These are used to hold your kabobs.

Substitute: Wire hangers that have been bent out straight first and then folded in half can be strong enough to hold any kabob. Or old metal handles off of fly swatters work great, too.

Smoke-free glasses: Thanks to these glasses you can BBQ without the bother of gettin' smoke in your eyes.

Substitute: You can run duct tape all around an old pair of glasses for the same effect. Also a pair of those tannin' goggles works pretty good on sunny days. And a scuba mask with the nose cut out will do just fine.

Water spray bottle: This item helps you to take control of any flare-ups that might take place without puttin' your entire cookin' fire out.

Substitute: See sauce spray bottle substitute.

MEET YOUR MEAT

Now, dear reader, there are books out there that'll actually tell you how to slaughter your meat before you BBQ it. Needless to say, you won't find that kind of stuff in here. "Why?" you might ask. Well, you see we trailer park folks barely got room enough in our yards to fit a car let alone a farm animal. I say this even though as I mentioned in my holiday cookbook as a small girl I raised a hog. But back then the trailer homes were much smaller then they are today. The trailer I grew up in was like a dang cracker box with tires. Because of its size, we had much more yard space where a small farm animal could live quite comfortably. Mind you, the rest of us were hunchbacks, but them farm animals were happy. So forget about the slaughterin' part, just get up and go to the dang Piggly Wiggly or Winn Dixie, for goodness sake.

Now, I ain't gonna tell you how to cook each piece of meat. Y'all ain't stupid; you bought this here book, didn't you? Surely you know that the meat goes on the BBQ and you turn it from time to time, stickin' a thermometer in it on occasion till the gauge reads the right temperature for the doneness that you like. That y'all already know. But I will give you some tips on what you should and should not do when cookin' your beef, pork, chicken, or fish. Tip number one is know what kind of beef product you're buyin'. Steaks are not all alike, so I've included a listin' that you'll find here in just a bit that will help you decide what part of the cow to buy. Tip number two, it never hurt any kind of meat to marinate for a bit. Marinade will change the taste and texture of your beef, pork, lamb, and chicken as will glazes, sauces, and rubs. But don't just settle for the ones you find in the store, take a look at Chapter 15. And last but not least, don't pierce your meat after you've set it on the grill. If all you got is a fork to turn your meat, then stab it in the fattiest part.

But before we get started BBQin' I want to talk to you about your meat. Have you ever had someone put your meat in their mouth only to spit it out and say, "Dang it, that's nasty?" Well, that could be on account of several different things. One could be that your meat is old. I can tell you now that nobody, regardless of how it's been prepared, wants to put old meat in their mouth. So if you got old meat, you might as well throw it away. Another reason could be on account of your meat bein' too hard. It's all right if your meat is firm, but nobody wants meat that's so hard if it should slip it could poke their eye out. Another reason could be on account of the way you bathe or prepare your meat. If your meat is crusty with a bad odor, forget about anybody touchin' it. But don't worry, dear reader, there are solutions to all these problems.

When you buy your meat, make sure you check the date on the sticker. If it's got today's date on it, don't buy it regardless of how good the price might be. Treat your meat like it was your milk. If the expiration date says today's date, more than likely you won't drink it. Just remember that there's a reason for those expiration dates. And when you buy your beef, make sure it's a dull to bright red, marbled with streaks of fat, and that it has a nice white fat outer coatin'. This will assure that your meat is juicy as well. Of course, before you slap your meat on the BBQ, you're goin' to trim off a lot of that outer fat so you don't start any flare-ups. You can cook the fatty pieces with some of the meat still on it over on another side of the grill away from your meat. Just whatever you do, don't throw it away, 'cause surely there's someone around your neighborhood who'd just love to eat your fatty meat.

As y'all know some meats are tough, but they can easily be tenderized. All you have to do is cut slits in your meat, put it in a marinade, and let it set for at least a day. This will do three things: tenderize it, add flavor, and reduce the cancer-causin' agent that can come from BBQin' your meat. And if you put your marinatin' meat in the fridge to do its thing, you can go all the way up to three or four days without needin' to cook it. Just make sure your meat is fresh and don't expire in three to four days. Now, all your meats can be marinated, but you know you will definitely need to marinate all shoulder steaks (English steak, London broil), top round steaks (top round London broil), eye round steaks (beef sirloin tip steak), skirt steaks (fajita meat, Philadelphia steak), chuck seven-bone steak (center chuck steak), and flank steaks (flank steak filet, London broil). So if your meat is too hard, soak it.

When we talk about bathin' your meat, we are referrin' to the marinatin' process that I went over. I've included some of our favorite marinades at the High Chaparral, but please feel free to come up with some of your own. Just be careful that you don't put ingredients in your bath that will make your meat smell or taste funny. There are some items that shouldn't be combined and you'll find out which ones those are as you experiment. But if you want to make a marinade that works, it must contain an acid that you might find in vinegar or apple juice or beer, salt, oil, and seasonin's.

A crust is produced on your meat when you use a rub to trap in your flavor and juice of your meat. I've included several of our favorite rubs as well. The good Lord knows that we like rubs. As a matter of fact I'm always happy and thrilled when my husband comes home from the Piggly Wiggly and asks me to rub his meat. It usually means he's goin' to be BBQin' some time in the near future. Just remember that a rub will not tenderize your meat. All it will do is make it more flavorful. So come on, dear reader, and rub your meat.

Last but not least, there is one type of meat that people always tend to have problems with when it comes to BBQin' and that is your wienie. For some reason, some of y'all have the worse times with your wienies. They're either ripped apart from getting' stuck, deformed or mangled, cold and limp, or even worse, the dang thing's fallin' through the cracks. Trust me when I tell y'all, nobody wants a burnt wienie. It just ain't right. Y'all need to spend more time and care with your wienies. These are precious pieces of meat that need your attention. The first thing to remember is to put your wienie on the grill so that it's runnin' the opposite way that the grill is runnin'. In other words, if the cracks on the grill are goin' side to side, then you want your wienie to go up and down for pleasurable results. And when it comes time to turn it, be careful with it. Don't grab hold of it with a pair of tongs like it's some old stick in the yard. And for goodness sake, don't stab your wienie with a knife. You don't want to pierce your wienie, 'cause you're likely to dry it out. Just remember that when your guest bites down on your wienie, you want it to be both flavorful and juicy in their mouths, not burnt and dry or saggy and limp. So please keep an eye on your wienie while BBQin', and also remember, if you don't want it to stick, lube it up with a coat of oil first.

BEFORE YOU START BBQIN'

One thing is for sure when it comes to BBQin' in the trailer world. Once you start cookin' everybody will find a reason to stop by. I think this is a trailer park thing. In the non-wheeled-home community your neighbors might be tempted to stop by your house, but they have better manners.

Well, in the wheeled-home community the neighbors don't give a flying hot dog bun what people think of 'em. You got BBQ? They're comin' over. That's why I'd like to suggest that you do the same thing I do when I cook out. Lay electrified barb wire all around your yard and turn the water sprinkler on low. Mind you, the first row of wire might not stop those un-invited dinner guest wannabes, but once they've hit the water sprinkler, the second row's voltage will knock 'em back to yesterday. It's amazin' how 220 volts of juice runnin' through a wet human bein' and the light smell of electrified flesh will make 'em forget what the heck they stopped by your trailer for.

Now, if you're usin' a charcoal BBQ, make sure to use your chimney starter. And also remember that the more lighter fluid you use, the worse your meat is gonna taste on account of all them there chemicals in that stuff. If you are usin' self-startin' charcoals, let 'em cook for a long time in order to burn out all that lighter fluid that they was presoaked in at the factory. Make sure your BBQ is away from your trailer, trees, or anythin' else that might catch on fire from the flames you might get when you're cookin'. Once you've done all this, strike that match.

If you're lightin' a gas grill, always raise the lid first before turnin' on the gas. Lord, I forgot about this one time and as soon as I hit the button to start the fire, there was a loud explosion, and my lid ended up way over on top the trailer in Lot #3. I tell you, folks, I was lucky I wasn't hurt. So unless you're that kid from that boy band who wanted to go into space, don't light your grill with the lid shut.

The last thing you should do before BBQin' your food is to oil down your grill. This is very important since it'll make sure your food don't stick thus you'll have a good cookin' experience. So just remember, dear reader, a lubed-up grill is a happy grill.

WHILE YOU'RE BBQIN'

Donna Sue, Momma Ballzak, and Faye Faye LaRue will all most likely dis-agree with me on this one, but, folks, you got a fire burnin' right in your front yard, so don't drink while you're BBQin'. The last thing I want is a drunk BBQin' my food, which is why when Donna Sue has meat on the grill, I got the pin on the fire extinguisher pulled and settin' right next to me. But like I said, some folks ain't gonna agree with me on this, and I respect what they say. But let me just add that there's a reason why Momma Ballzak wears a wig, and the reason ain't for fashion.

NOW THAT YOU'RE DONE

Now, many folks will tell you that the best thing about BBQin' is the great outdoors flavor it gives the food, or the tenderness it adds to the meat, or even the ultimate satisfaction that a person gets from cookin' the same way Adam and Eve did. All that is good and well, but in the trailer park world, the best thing about BBQin' is the fact that you don't have to clean anything. Yes, we know you should always clean your grill when you've finished cookin', but so what if it waits till mornin' or next week. Kenny and Donny from Lot #15 insist on cleanin' everythin' right then and there while Anita Biggon in Lot # 2 will wait till the next day or two before takin' a water hose and a wire brush to hers. Why, my husband, Dew's momma, Momma Ballzak, of Lot #16 has had the same kettle grill for forty some odd years and has yet to touch it with a cleanin' product. All she does is light the coals and when they get to that point where they're ready for cookin', she pours a little bit of rum or Everclear over the areas of the grill that she plans to use. Of course, this causes a big flame that lasts until the alcohol has burnt off. Once the flame has died down and she's had a few cocktails, she puts her food on the grill for what she claims to be safe cookin'. Accordin' to Momma Ballzak, "If that don't kill them germs, nothin' will." I think she may be right.

Chapter 3

Who'd have guessed we'd find such a good use for them pants and shirt that one of Donna Sue's male visitors up and left when he sobered up the next day and flew out of her trailer like an empty vodka bottle on a Saturday night? By the way, yard statue theft has dropped 80 percent at the High Chaparral Trailer Park since this photo was taken.

How to Decorate the Trailer Park for a BBQ

As I've said many times already, individually we BBQ year-round. When it's just me and my husband or some friends or even family cookin' out for a meal, we don't spend any time or money on decoratin' our trailer. We'd rather take that cash and spend it on a good piece of meat or upgrade to a better level of ground beef. But when all the lots come together for one of our many trailer park BBQs, we get out-and-out festive with our decorations. But of course this don't mean that we break the bank. Oh, heck no! Instead we just get creative. Now I know that there are some of you who either ain't all that creative or don't have time to sit around and come up with festive decorations for your upcomin' BBQ gatherin', so me and the gang at the High Chaparral Trailer Park have decided to share with you some of our very own ideas and tips. So get your marker and get ready to highlight, 'cause it's time for Trailer Park BBQ Decoratin' 101.

Now, I'll tell you that since I've become a star, I try to pitch in a bit by addin' a little reward for all those who've worked hard makin' the BBQ party look real good and fun. For example, I had my husband, Dew, and Kyle Chitwood of Lot #11 go pick up a couple of kegs at Beaver Liquor. Needless to say, when they unloaded those kegs of beer off the truck, you should have heard everyone's excitement. The boys set the kegs up behind the office. That way people could walk back there by themselves, come out a few minutes later, and still be a good Baptist. Naturally Sister Bertha threw a fit and was up in arms. But the case of A & W root beer that Dew, my husband, pulled out from the front seat shut her up but good. There ain't nothin' Sister Bertha likes more than a cold A & W unless it's a fried pickle. Anyways, gettin' back to the beer, Ben Beaver gave us the kegs for the regular price of $5.29 each, includin' cups. Now, that ain't bad for a premium beer like Old Milwaukee, or so I'm told. Of course we had to leave a $250 deposit on each keg and pump, but, hey, that's just good business practice is what the heck that is.

But if you do want to go all out and decorate your trailer park for a big BBQ, it's pretty easy. Let's start with the heavy items first. Give your BBQ a more homey quality by puttin' a few bales of hay out around the area where y'all are plannin' on eatin'. These will make your event feel rural regardless of where y'all might live. Plus they make great comfortable seats. And even after the BBQ is finished, y'all can make a trailer park scarecrow security guard to set out in your front gate in the evenin'. All you need is a spare pillowcase (since this is goin' to be his face, it's best that you not use one with flowers or prints on it), an old shirt, a pair of your husband's pants (if he's been a pain lately, make 'em a pair of his favorite pants), a pair of gloves, and a hat of some kind. You'll also need a stapler. Just stuff each item of clothin' with the hay, and then staple 'em all together. Of course, the hat will just be placed on the stuffed head-shaped pillow and then stapled. Take a flashlight or, if you got an electrical outlet over by the main gate entrance, get a floodlight and rig it up to your scarecrow's arms so it's shinin' outward and away from him. Set him up by the main gate, draw on a mean-lookin' face with a marker, and relax in your trailer knowin' that those pesky thugs that like to sneak into your trailer park and steal your plastic and cement yard statues ain't comin' in for a while. Well, at least the dumber ones won't be botherin' you too soon.

Next, try and round up some wagon wheels. You can find these out in old barns and other places where wagons might have been. If you can't find wagon wheels, just take some tires off the top of your roof and throw those around where y'all gather. And if the weather won't permit you to take the tires off your roof, then just grab the jack, the tire iron, and some cinder blocks, and take 'em right off your car, preferably the one that ain't runnin' right now.

Special lights for late afternoon and evenin' BBQs can really add that special "Hey, we're cookin' over here" feelin' to the atmosphere. Save those flat Styrofoam plates that your meat usually is packed in. Wash these real good and then dry 'em off. Next wrap 'em up in foil. Take a sharp knife and carefully poke little holes about a half inch apart through both the foil and the plates. Take a small set of those tiny outdoor Christmas lights and gently push one light through each hole. Attach string and hang these up on tree branches, sides of your wall, or wherever you can find to suspend 'em. And once you plug 'em in, you'll see that these lovely little special tea lights are perfect for makin' this BBQ even more extraordinary than the rest. Plus if you save these, you can top your Christmas tree with one, or use it as an emergency gift when you realize you've forgotten your mother in-law's birthday again. Plus these also make great outdoor floodlights if you change the twinkle lights to the larger Christmas lights, and string 'em across the driveway. Not only does it add everyday beauty to what might be a not-so-beautiful trailer home, but your husband can also use 'em as emergency lightin' when he's workin' on your car. This also assures that regardless of the time of day, that old son of a gun ain't got no excuse not to mow the lawn.

Another great use for those Christmas twinkle lights is to pair 'em with them individual aluminum cupcake holders. Poke a hole in each one and easily slide the lights in. Just a word of warnin', don't string these up around the BBQ itself, even if it does look pretty. The last thing you need is a $20 BBQ grill with a $3 strand of Christmas lights melted permanently onto it. Keep these lovely things away from fire and/or heat.

Another thing that's fun is to get some of this new Spirit Foam, which has just recently come out on the market, and write out cute sayin's on your trailer. It's both safe and fun, and it won't hurt you or your trailer home. You can write things like

"Make Mine Rare."
"I'll Take a Big One."
"Come On, Baby, Light My Fire."
"Forget Charcoal, We Got Gas."
"I Got the Best Sauce in Town."

Just let your imagination go wild. And the good thing about this Spirit Foam is that after it's dry, you can just peel it right off and throw it away. Ain't that just nice?

Take a paper plate and glue charcoals on it to make a smiley face as another decoration. It only takes eight coals: two for the eyes, one for the nose, and five for the smile. Make several of these and you can hang 'em up around the cookin' area or on each trailer. Just be careful and make sure you don't use the self-lightin' kind. The last thing you want is to lose a trailer 'cause some farsighted woodpecker got sparks flyin' with its beak and that self-lightin' charcoal. Also make sure you hang your coal man up high. You don't want to lose him on account of a cheap neighbor who's in the mood to BBQ, either.

And last but not least is to brighten the occasion up with personalized wienie sticks. Nothin' says "let's party" like holdin' your wienie at a cookout or, better yet, a church retreat. You can make this possible by goin' out and cuttin' down enough branches from a tree (preferably from your neighbor's tree) for you and the rest of the folks who'll be in attendance. Whittle down one end to a fine point, then take your brightest nail polish and write each person's name on the end of the stick. Make sure it ain't flammable or somebody's gonna have a hot scorched wienie. Feel free to use these personalized wienie sticks for roastin' your marshmallows later on.

Well, dear reader, thanks to these few simple decoratin' tidbits, your group BBQ will not only smell and taste good, but it will look good as well. And if you come up with other ideas that you'd like to share with me and your fellow readers, please come and visit my Web pages at www. rubyann.org, and add your hints to my message board.

Chapter 4

While Mickey Ray Kay enjoys a Dr Pepper and his wife Connie Kay looks on in disbelief, his momma Wanda Kay attempts for the first and last time to eat an appetizer directly off the BBQ. Sometimes the mind just slips, don't it?

Appetizers

As y'all know by now, there really ain't no place for appetizers in a trailer park since we eat while we cook. Typically if we're gonna have potato skins or cheese sticks, we'll just eat those right along with the meat loaf and taters as part of our meal. But with BBQin' there just ain't no way to sample what your makin' while it's cookin', and if you doubt what I'm sayin', just ask Wanda Kay over in Lot #13. God bless her, she still has to draw her eyebrows on to this day. So as you can imagine, appetizers really come into play with this style of good old down-home cuisine.

With all the above said, I got to come back and tell y'all that even in BBQin' we don't think of appetizers in the same light as y'all do. You see, when you look it up in a dictionary, it says that they're "a food served usually before a meal to stimulate the appetite." Well, I can tell you right now that the only thing we need to stimulate our appetite at the High Chaparral Trailer Park is air comin' into our lungs. Trust me, folks, once we wake up in the mornin' or early afternoon, we're stimulated. Why there have been times I've been stimulated all day long. Tryin' to find an appetite has never been a problem in our trailer park, which is why we really get into appetizers while we BBQ. We eat these food items that're featured in this chapter while we're cookin' so that we don't get faint from hunger and pass out onto the grill. These foods are more along the line of emergency foods. In other words, we eat tons of dips, spreads, crackers, and the like—purely for health reasons. Oh, if only we had that luxury that some of y'all have and could actually bite down into one of them Armadillo Eggs just to enjoy the taste. Yes, if only I had the freedom to stick my chip in the Whipped Italian Dip for pleasure. It's a curse, folks. Yes, it's a curse that many of us trailer folks have to face each day. I wish that a telethon could help, 'cause I'd start one up today, but no, I'm sure that this plague of havin' to constantly eat between meals is somethin' that even modern medicine, with all its scientific breakthroughs, will never be able to conquer. It's somethin' that we folks have had to live with all our lives and will continue to deal with day in and day out. And of course, we don't want your pity. Oh no, we simply want your understandin'. So next time you see a friend eat a bag of cookies, or a pint or more of ice cream, or a whole box of Ritz crackers, don't make fun of 'em or call 'em a cow or pig. But just stop and think that maybe they are just like me or my sister or the other folks at the High Chaparral Trailer Park. Yes, maybe, dear reader, that person sittin' next to you with chocolate frostin' and tiny pieces of yellow cake crumbs all over their face, maybe, possibly they're just stimulated.

ARMADILLO EGGS

These tasty treats are real big at the Taco Tackle Shack and, thanks to Lois and Hubert Bunch, at all our trailer park BBQs as well.

Makes 20 jalapeños

20 jalapeño peppers, cut in half and seeded
½ pound Velveeta cheese
1 pound bulk sausage, browned and crumbled
40 slices bacon

Fill each jalapeño half with Velveeta, then put 'em back together, mold the sausage around the jalapeños, and wrap with two slices of bacon. BBQ on the grill till bacon is cooked, turnin' often.

—Lois Bunch, Lot #3

MISSIONARY DIP

Just recently Pastor Ida May Bee began holdin' a thirty-minute meetin' with chips and dip just before the evenin' service on the first Sunday of every month so that we folks can become more informed on the missionary position as well as other positions that people in the church can take on. Even though they left at the end of the meetin' lookin' a bit disappointed, my sister, Donna Sue, and neighbor Faye Faye LaRue did make it to the first meetin'. I don't know if they actually felt like they had a callin' to that position or if they simply came, like the rest of us, for this dip that Pastor Ida May promised she'd serve. So far none of us has volunteered to take on the position of missionary, but we have got a few new ushers and a bell ringer.

Makes 3 to 3 ½ cups

1 regular can kernel corn
1 large red onion, diced
1 tomato, diced
1 red bell pepper, diced
1 yellow bell pepper, diced
4 tablespoons lime juice
4 tablespoons chopped cilantro
2 teaspoons olive oil
1 teaspoon salt
½ teaspoon cayenne pepper
Dash of black pepper

Mix everything up and serve with salty corn chips. This stuff gets even better if you cover it and put it in the fridge for a day.

—*Pastor Ida May Bee, Lot #7*

WHIPPED ITALIAN DIP

Every day between four and five Tina Faye offers a happy hour for all her hotel guests out by the pool. Anyways, this dip is the highlight of that hour, especially since she ain't got a liquor license.

Makes about 1½ cups

½ cup ground pepperoni
3 ounces cream cheese, softened

2 tablespoons chopped parsley
¼ cup whipped cream
Dash of Italian seasonin'

Usin' a mixer, combine the pepperoni, cream cheese, and parsley. Fold in the whipped cream and then add the seasonin'. Place in a bowl and serve with chips or crackers.

—*Tina Faye Stopenblotter, Lot #17*

KITTY CHITWOOD'S HUSSY SPREAD

Once again, Kitty is at it with the leftover beer recipes. I swear, with all the beer they go through in that trailer of theirs, you'd think they was Lutherans.

Makes 2 ½ cups

2 cups shredded Velveeta cheese
3 ounces cream cheese, softened
1 tablespoon minced garlic
½ teaspoon salt
¼ teaspoon pepper
⅛ teaspoon hot sauce
⅓ cup beer
1 tablespoon minced parsley

Put all the ingredients except the beer and parsley in a large bowl. Blend 'em all together and then add your beer a little at a time. It may not take all of your beer, so watch the thickness of the mixture. You want to be able to spread it on bread or crackers, not eat it with a spoon. Once you've gotten it to a nice thickness, put it into a servin' bowl and sprinkle the parsley on top. Cover and place in the fridge to sit overnight. Take out of the fridge right around 30 minutes before servin'. This is good on crackers, or you can spread some on sliced pieces of bread and put 'em on the BBQ to heat up.

—*Kitty Chitwood, Lot #11*

ST. PETER'S WALKIN'-ON-WATER DIP

Lord, I don't know where Sister Bertha comes up with her recipe names.

Makes about 1½ cups

8 ounces cream cheese, softened
1 tablespoon minced onion
4 tablespoons French dressin'
4 tablespoons ketchup

Mix all together, say a prayer, and serve with chips.

—*Sister Bertha, Lot #12*

MOMMA BALLZAK'S REAL FUN SPREAD

If she could remember where she put her rubber stamp and ink pad, Donna Sue would give this recipe her stamp of approval.

Makes 1 cup

½ pound finely shredded Velveeta cheese
1½ ounces dry sherry
1 tablespoon brandy
⅛ teaspoon Worcestershire sauce

In a large bowl, cream your first three ingredients together. Add the Worcestershire sauce and cream again. Cover and put in the fridge overnight. This will last about a month. Use it with crackers.

—*Momma Ballzak, Lot #16*

TACO TACKLE SHACK'S EL GRANDE COJONES

These sound bigger than they are.

Makes about 75 balls

½ pound Velveeta cheese, finely chopped
3 ounces cream cheese, softened
½ clove garlic, crushed
¼ cup chili powder

Mix your first three ingredients together until well blended. Roll into marble-size balls. Then roll the balls in the chili powder. Put each ball on a wax paper–covered cookie sheet, cover, and place in the fridge to chill. These last about a week in the fridge or even longer if you freeze 'em.

—Lois Bunch, Lot #3

SOUTH OF THE BORDER DIP

This was one of the recipes Fernando left behind when immigration came and hauled his behind away.

Makes 3 to 4 cups

1 pound Velveeta cheese, cut into cubes
1 small can chiles
1 regular package taco seasonin'
1 regular can Cheddar cheese soup

Put all this in a big bowl and microwave until the Velveeta melts completely. Stir every three minutes while cookin'. Take it out of the microwave and give it a good stirrin'. Serve in a bowl with tortilla chips.

—Fernando Diaz, Formely of Lot #1

VANCE POOL'S SPICE NUTS

Donna Sue, who just loves nuts and will go any where to get 'em, says that after samplin' all over this area, she can guarantee that Vance has the "hottest nuts in town."

Makes 1½ cups

1 cup sugar
½ cup boilin' water
2 teaspoons cayenne pepper
½ teaspoon cinnamon
⅛ teaspoon cream of tartar
1½ cups peanuts, shelled
½ teaspoon vanilla

Mix the first five ingredients together, put on the stove, and bring it up to a boil. When it reaches 245 degrees F., add the peanuts followed by the vanilla. Stir until well blended and then spoon the nuts out onto wax paper. Quickly spread the nuts out into one layer and let 'em cool. Keep nuts in an airtight container and away from children.

—*Vance Pool, Lot #19*

KENNY'S CRAB MOUSSE

I can't find it in my heart to eat this. I don't care for seafood and I loved Bullwinkle.

Makes about 3 cups

1½ packets unflavored gelatin
¼ cup cold water
8 ounces cream cheese, softened
1 regular can cream of mushroom soup
⅔ cup mayonnaise
1 regular can crabmeat
½ cup celery, finely chopped

½ cup green onions, chopped
1 teaspoon curry powder

Put your gelatin in your water and let it dissolve. Then use an electric mixer to whip the cream cheese, soup, and mayonnaise. Cover and put in the fridge for an hour. Take it out and mix in the crabmeat, celery, onions, and curry powder. Take the mixer and whip all this up once more. Now, if y'all are eatin' it inside, go ahead and put this in a mold that you've already applied a coatin' of cookin' spray to. If y'all are goin' to eat it outside, just put it in a servin' dish or a bowl. Regardless, place it in the fridge again for around 2 hours. Serve with your favorite crackers or French bread.

—Kenny Lynn, Lot #15

Chapter 5

For some unknown reason, after Harland Hix got out of the hospital recently, he up and switched from a charcoal BBQ to a gas one.

Beef

As I mentioned earlier in this here book, I ain't goin' to take the time to tell you how to cook a steak or a burger or anythin' like that on a BBQ. Y'all already know how to turn a piece of meat, and by usin' a thermometer, you should be able to cook your beef cut to the perfect doneness that you and your guests like. I will tell y'all how to make a brisket since that one seems to be a problem for a lot of people out there. Y'all either get it tough, or it comes out dry, or in some cases, there ain't much difference between your brisket and the briquettes below it. So don't worry, I got the queen of the briskets at the High Chaparral Trailer Park to give me her brisket recipe.

You'll also notice that there are a lot of recipes for hamburgers in this chapter. Well, the reason for this is on account of it bein' cheap and common. But if you're like me, I get tired of the same old kind of burger each and every day. So without goin' crazy and doin' somethin' like usin' turkey burger meat instead (now that just ain't Christian), we simply decided to share with you some of the favorite burger recipes. I know these are goin' to be the answer to your prayers.

LAST STOP NURSING HOME FILET MIGNON

The fine folks up at the Last Stop Nursing Home over by the last stop till you get to the boat docks sent this recipe with Me-Ma when we went and picked her up one day. Boy, she just loves these on account that she can chew 'em.

Makes 4 servin's

2 pounds hamburger meat
1 teaspoon garlic powder
1 teaspoon onion powder

½ teaspoon salt
Dash of pepper
8 strips bacon
Worcestershire sauce

Mix the hamburger and seasonin's together, then shape into 4 round patties. Wrap 2 bacon strips around each patty, usin' toothpicks to hold 'em on. BBQ, carefully flippin' occasionally until done. Leave 'em on the grill and put a little Worcestershire sauce on top of each one, close the BBQ lid, and let 'em cook for 1½ minutes more, or until nice and brown on top.

—*Last Stop Nursing Home*

CONNIE'S TASTY PATTIES

Connie uses these as a weapon. She throws some patties on the BBQ, and when you stop by to see what that wonderful smell is, she gladly offers you one in exchange for an order from one of the many product lines that she sells. Why, I could moisturize the entire state of Arkansas with all the extra bottles of Skin So Soft I've got in my bathroom. I tell you, she's evil!

Makes 6 to 8 good-size patties

8 ounces tomato sauce
1 cup ketchup
1 cup crackers or bread crumbs
1 cup chopped onions
1 egg, beaten
2½ teaspoons salt
2 teaspoons Worcestershire sauce
1 teaspoon liquid smoke
3 tablespoons brown sugar
2 pounds hamburger meat

Combine all the ingredients together with your hands like you do with a meat loaf. Make sure everythin' is mixed together real good. Form into patties and place on the grill. Baste these with Tina Faye's Burger Glaze on page 148. Cook until they reach the desired doneness that you like. You can eat them as they are or on a bun. Personally I like to top them with my Sweet Sauce that you'll find on page 143. They are good with any sauce or just by themselves.

—Connie Kay, Lot #13

DONNA SUE'S PATTY MELT

One bite of this and you'll swear Donna Sue's done patty melts all her life.

Makes 6 burgers

2 teaspoons margarine plus more to coat the bread
1 cup chopped onion
12 slices rye bread
2 pounds hamburger meat
Salt and pepper to taste
12 slices Swiss cheese
¾ cup Thousand Island dressin'

Take a small skillet and put it on your BBQ grill. Add the 2 teaspoons margarine and let it melt, then follow this by addin' the onions. Let the onions cook for a minute or two, or until they get slightly brown. Set the skillet off the grill and let the onions continue to cook in the hot margarine, stirrin' every so often.

Next spread one side of each slice of bread with margarine and place, spread side down, on a cookie sheet. Put the cookie sheet on the grill and toast until one side is golden brown. Take the cookie sheet off the grill and wrap the bread up in foil to keep it warm. Set aside.

Divide the hamburger meat and shape into six ½-inch-thick patties that are about as big as your bread slices. Cook the patties until they're done to your likin', flippin' each one occasionally. Add your salt and pepper. Top each burger with an equal share of the browned onions, followed by a slice of cheese. Next add a slice of rye bread, toasted side up, on top of the cheese. Carefully flip this over and quickly add an equal share of Thousand Island dressin' to the exposed bottom of the burger. Then just as quickly, place the remainin' slice of rye bread, toasted side up, on top of the dressin'. Once again carefully flip the sandwich, let it grill for 10 seconds, and take it off the BBQ. (If you find that you keep burnin' your bread when you try to put it on the burger, simply put your bottom slice on a piece of foil, toasted side down. Add your dressin' to this. Put your other slice of bread, toasted side up, on the onioned-and-cheesed patty. Holdin' on to the top slice of bread, carefully take your burger off the BBQ and place it on the slice of bread with the dressin' on it. Now use that foil to wrap up your sandwich tightly. Place this on the BBQ and let it grill for another 3 to 4 minutes on each side before servin'.) Throw in a pickle and you got yourself a good time.

—Donna Sue Boxcar, Lot #6

URI KROCHICHIN'S BORIS YELTSIN TRIBUTE BEEF BBQ

Don't let the name fool you, there is absolutely no vodka used in this dish.

Makes 6 servin's

5 pounds sirloin or flank steak, with the fat trimmed off
2 green bell peppers, seeded and cut into strips
½ head green cabbage, shredded
3 carrots, shredded
2 onions, sliced
1 regular can bean sprouts, drained
1½ cups soy sauce
9 cups water
½ cup cornstarch
¼ cup toasted sesame seeds
2 tablespoons sugar
1 tablespoon crushed red pepper flakes
6 pita breads
4 cups cooked white rice

Take your beef and slice it into real thin strips. Set aside.

Get your veggies ready and set them aside as well.

Usin' your grill wok or a pan, add your soy sauce, water, cornstarch, sesame seeds, sugar, and crushed red pepper flakes. Mix well and let it get hot but not boilin'. Take it off the grill and pour half of this sauce into a bowl and put that in the fridge. Take the rest that you got in the grill wok and set aside.

For this recipe, you're gonna need to be usin' that grill top. Place the veggies on the BBQ first and let 'em cook on one side. Baste these with the sauce from the grill wok. Turn your veggies, baste again, and put your meat on the BBQ. Keep a real close eye on your beef and keep bastin' it. Since it's sliced thin, it'll cook up real fast. Once everythin' is cooked, take a pita, cut it in half, and load each half with a few spoons of rice, some veggies, and 3 or 4 slices of beef. Serve with a bottle of soy sauce so folks can add more if they like.

—*Uri Krochichin, Lot #1*

POOR MAN'S STEAK

Call 'em what you want, these babies go fast.

Makes about 4 patties

1 cup corn flakes, crushed
1 egg
¼ cup BBQ sauce
1 teaspoon salt
⅛ teaspoon pepper
1 pound hamburger meat

Put the cereal, egg, BBQ sauce, salt, and pepper all in a large bowl and mix well. Next, add the hamburger and mix with your hands until it is combined. Shape into patties, brush with more BBQ sauce, and grill like you would hamburgers till they're done to your likeness.

—*Juanita Hix, Lot #9*

BAPTIST BURGERS

Eatin' one of these will not get you to heaven, it'll only taste like you're there.

Makes 8 to 10 burgers

½ cup ketchup
½ cup Worcestershire sauce
½ cup minced onions
1½ teaspoons salt
1 teaspoon pepper
3 pounds hamburger meat

Mix all the ingredients minus the hamburger together in a large bowl. Fold in the hamburger with your hands until everythin' is mixed up real good. Shape into thick patties and BBQ until they get to the desired doneness. Feel free to throw some Velveeta cheese on top of 'em if you like cheeseburgers. These will be very juicy.

—*Pastor Ida May Bee, Lot #7*

LOVIE BIRCH'S BBQ PARTY BURGERS

We sure will miss the Birches. I know Momma just broke down in tears when she heard the news, 'cause she just loves Elmer and Lovie, and Lovie's BBQ party burgers. Don't worry Momma, I swiped the recipe when I went over to give Lovie a goin'-away ham loaf.

Makes 8 burgers

8 ounces sour cream
¼ cup mayonnaise
½ package dried onion soup mix
⅜ cup bread crumbs
¼ teaspoon salt
¼ teaspoon pepper
2½ pounds hamburger meat
8 hamburger buns

Mix everythin' but the buns together, stirrin' after each item is added until well blended. When you get to the meat, mix it all together with your hands. Form into 8 patties and place on the BBQ. Cook on each side until they get to the doneness that you like. Place on buns and serve.

—*Lovie Birch, Lot #20*

LOVIE'S LONDON BROIL BABIES

Now don't let the ingredients scare you, 'cause this sandwich is good.

Makes 4 sandwiches

2 pounds London broil, already rubbed with your favorite rub
    (see pages 56–63)
½ cup hot sauce
½ cup white vinegar
1 teaspoon garlic powder
½ teaspoon salt
¼ teaspoon onion powder
⅛ teaspoon white pepper
⅛ teaspoon black pepper
⅛ teaspoon crushed red pepper
4 hoagie rolls

Place your meat on the BBQ. While one side of it cooks, combine all the remainin' ingredients minus the rolls together. Mix well. Brush this mixture on the uncooked side of the meat. Turn your meat over and brush the top side now. Baste the meat every time you turn it until it gets to the doneness that you desire. Take the meat off the BBQ and slice it into very thin slices. Divide the slices into 4 piles and place 'em on the grill. (Top with your favorite cheese, and onions if you like. Once the cheese has melted, take the meat off the BBQ and onto a hoagie roll.) Serve with your favorite BBQ sauce.

—*Lovie Birch, Lot #20*

EL WIENIE MEXICANO

This recipe that I picked up durin' a recent trip to New Mexico is a Hispanic version of what some folks know as a pig in a blanket.

Makes 8

8 wienies
1 package taco seasonin'
½ tablespoon margarine, melted
8 tortillas
1 cup salsa
1 cup sour cream
1 cup Velveeta cheese, shredded
1 cup green or red chiles, diced
1 sliced jalapeño pepper

Put your wienies on the BBQ, give 'em a light spray of water, and sprinkle 'em with some taco seasonin'. Each time you turn the wienies, give 'em another sprinklin' of taco seasonin'. Cook until they are done to your likeness. When you take the wienies off the BBQ, carefully lay a large sheet of foil on the grill. Brush on a light layer of melted margarine on each side of the tortillas and place 'em on the sheet of foil. Let 'em cook for about 30 seconds to 1 minute, then turn. Take 'em off the BBQ and place a wienie on each one. Add 1 or 2 tablespoons of salsa, and sour cream, followed by some Velveeta, a spoonful of chiles, and a few slices of jalapeño. Roll each tortilla up and wrap it in wax paper and foil till you're ready to eat.

—Ruby Ann Boxcar, Lot #18

PASTOR IDA MAY BEE'S BIBLE BELT BRISKET

We might not be able to dance, but look what we get to eat. By the way, this recipe will only work with a gas BBQ.

Makes 5 to 7 pounds untrimmed brisket

5 to 7 pounds brisket, with the fat on
3 batches Sister Bertha's Revival Rub (page 161)
1 batch Dr Pepper Marinade (page 154)

Take your brisket and pierce it in several places on all the sides. Place it on a sheet of butcher paper or foil that's big enough to completely cover the meat, but you ain't ready to cover it yet. Take the rub and rub it all over your meat. Wrap the paper or foil completely around the meat and put in the fridge for 2 hours.

While the meat is in the fridge, make up the batch of marinade. At the end of the 2 hours, take the meat out and open up the paper or foil. If you used butcher's paper or you messed your foil up when openin' it, transfer your meat over to a piece of heavy duty foil that's just as big. Next, take the foil and loosely wrap the meat, leavin' the top completely open. You should have what looks like a big foil dish with a piece of meat in it. Now pour the marinade over the brisket, close the foil tightly at the top, place the whole thing in a pan, and place in the fridge to set overnight. Before you go off to bed, flip the foiled brisket over.

Light up your BBQ first thing in the mornin' and get it to a temperature of 225 degrees F. Take out your pan and wrapped brisket from the fridge and walk it to your BBQ. If you see that it's lost some of its juice, carefully reopen the top portion of the foil and pour it back in. Go ahead and take your foiled brisket out of the pan and set it with the fat side up (if you don't recall which side is the fat side, go ahead and take another peek, but put that foil back on) directly on the BBQ grill. Close the BBQ lid and take the pan back to the trailer with you. The juices in the foil will help to keep the meat juicy. You're goin' to cook this brisket for 9 hours without openin' the lid. You will need to go out and check every so often that the temperature stays at around 225 degrees F. When you've reached that 9-hour mark, go on out and turn your brisket over and cook for another hour. Before you take that thing off the grill at the end of its cookin' time, stick a thermometer in it and make sure it's done. So if you start your brisket on the BBQ about seven or eight in the mornin', then it should be done just in time for supper. Make sure you say grace before eatin', and remember those poor people in other parts of this world who ain't got this recipe and have to eat old dried-up shoe-leather–like brisket instead.

—*Pastor Ida May Bee, Lot #7*

KITTY'S ANYTIME ONION BURGERS

Your breath will be a lethal weapon, but, brother, what a way to die.

Makes 10 burgers

3 pounds of ground round
1 package dry onion soup mix
2 beef bouillon cubes, crushed
1 teaspoon garlic salt
½ teaspoon lemon pepper
½ teaspoon salt
⅛ teaspoon cayenne pepper
2 tablespoons beer
Grilled onions
10 hamburger buns

In a large bowl, mix everythin' but the grilled onions and buns together. Make into 10 patties and put on the grill. Cook each side for about 4 minutes to start. Check the doneness with a thermometer and cook until it gets to how you like it. When the patties are finished, place on the buns and top with the grilled onions. Enjoy, and have some mints nearby.

—*Kitty Chitwood, Lot #11*

TRAILER PARK MEAT MIX

This and a bag of chips, and you got a party goin' on!

Makes 4 to 6 servin's

1 tablespoon margarine
1 cup chopped onions
2 pounds ground beef
2 teaspoons salt
Dash of pepper
1½ cups ketchup
½ cup water
3 tablespoons sugar
2 tablespoons mustard
2 tablespoons vinegar
3 teaspoons Worcestershire sauce

Put your grill wok on the BBQ and drop your margarine into it. Melt the margarine and then add your onions, lettin' 'em grill for about 5 minutes, or until tender. Crumble up your beef and add it to the grill wok. You want to make sure that this doesn't form a patty, but rather it stays crumbled. Add your salt and pepper. Let cook.

While your meat is cookin', mix all the remainin' ingredients together in a bowl. Mix well. Set aside.

Once your meat is browned all the way through, add the ketchup mixture that you just made and stir it in real good. Let it cook until it all heats up. Serve with chips or on a bun.

—*Wanda Kay, Lot #13*

BALLZAK BURGERS

Accordin' to my husband's mother, Momma Ballzak, these tasty burgers have been handed down from Ballzak to Ballzak for many years. I have a feelin' the recipe was written on an empty liquor bottle, and I mean that in the nicest way possible.

Makes 6 burgers

½ tablespoon margarine
3 teaspoons cognac
1 teaspoon hot sauce
1 pound Velveeta cheese, cubed
2 pounds hamburger meat
1 teaspoon salt
½ teaspoon pepper
6 hamburger buns

Combine the first four ingredients in a bowl and stick it in the microwave. Cook till the cheese melts, stirrin' every so often. Stir well, set aside, and let it get cool.

Divide the meat into 6 equal portions. Then divide each of those portions in half. Shape the portions into 12 patties and make an indention in 6 of them. Scoop out 1 or 2 tablespoons of the cooled thickened Velveeta mixture and put it in the indentions. Top each of these patties with one of the non-cheesed patties. Make sure the sides are patted together to form a tight seal so none of the mixture runs out while cookin'. Put the patties on the grill and cook. When they are done to your likeness, top with the remainin' Velveeta mixture and serve on buns.

—*Momma Ballzak, Lot #16*

Chapter 6

The "So Long Birches" BBQ gave the High Chapparal Trailer Park Quiltin'
Club a chance to pose for one last photo with its original members before Lovie
and her husband moved away. Standing, from left to right, are Kenny Lynn,
Anita Biggon, Lulu Bell Boxcar, Lois Bunch, Sister Bertha, Juanita Hix, and
Donny Owens. Settin' in front are Lovie Birch, Momma Boxcar, and Dottie
Lamb.

Pork

As you know, I kind of touched on the topic of early BBQin' at the High Chaparral Trailer Park and what it was like. I talked about how some folks would rig up these makeshift BBQ grills and such, but I didn't really get into the days that my sister, Donna Sue, tells me about. You know the days back when she was a little girl, and I wasn't even around yet. I mean, way way way back when. Anyways, one of earliest memories as a little girl, and I got to just say that I was surprised she could remember yesterday, let alone fifty-some-odd years back, was when the menfolk of the park would build a great big hole out by where the swimmin' pool now sets. And they'd get a big fire burnin' in there real good and hot. Then while the ladies were preparin' the large pieces of pork that'd be cooked, the men would take the trailer park's swing set and remove all the seats. To hear my sister tell it, they'd attach big hooks on the ends of those chains where the seats used to be and then hook those pieces of pork on and let 'em dangle over the fire. Of course, the ladies would light up their cigarettes and get the cards out while the menfolk would talk about the weather, drink whatever they was able to sneak over to the pit without the women seein' 'em, and play with their meat. It was a gay time at the trailer park in those days.

When I asked my momma about those memories of Donna Sue's, she just giggled and assured me that I didn't miss out on nothin'. She said that what my sister forgot to mention was that the heat from the fire and weight of the meat made that swing set bend in two, and then the meat burnt, the grass by the pit caught on fire, and the men were too drunk to stomp it out. The women had to come over there with garden hoses and extinguish the grass fire. They only tried that pit thing one time. Momma does add that the only good thing that came out of that was the fact that after the rains had filled that pit with water, folks in the park used to go wadin' in it. It wasn't much, but it sure beat the heat.

Gay or not, I think these times in the trailer park are pretty good considerin' that we got these big ol' gas grills and a swimmin' pool. Of course we have to share it with the snakes.

THE DRUNKEN PIG

Go, Razorbacks!

Makes 4 servin's

2 tablespoons margarine
¾ teaspoon oregano
Juice of 1 lemon
1 tablespoon pepper
½ cup gin
4 pork chops

In a grillin' pan, melt the margarine, then add the oregano and lemon juice followed by the pepper. Stir. Slowly add the gin and stir the mixture often. Once it has heated up, add those pork chops and coat 'em with the warm mixture. Close the BBQ cover and let stand for 15 minutes on each side, bastin' the chops with the sauce ever 5 minutes. Serve on a plate with the sauce.
—*Momma Ballzak, Lot #16*

DONNA SUE'S LOINS

Be careful, folks, if not done right, these tend to be all dried out and nasty.

Makes 4 servin's

1 (4- to 5-pound) pork loin
1 cup water

2 ounces whiskey
1 batch Prancin' Pig Glaze (page 148)

Take your pork loin and semi wrap it up in heavy duty foil, leavin' the top open. Pour in your water and whiskey, seal the top tightly, place it on the BBQ over medium heat, and cook for an hour. Open the foil and glaze the pork loin with the glaze. Let it cook for another 15 minutes. Check for a internal temperature of 160 degrees F. Take off of the BBQ and slice. Serve with the glaze or your favorite BBQ sauce.

—Donna Sue Boxcar, Lot #6

THE SALSA SOW

Now, this would make Jimmy Dean squeal.

Makes 4 servin's

2 tablespoons Crisco
4 pork chops, boneless
1 batch Little Piggy Rub (page 162)
2 cups Velveeta cheese, shredded
1½ cups salsa

Grease up your pig with Crisco and sprinkle on the rub. Let the chops set for a few hours in a plastic bag in the fridge. The longer the better. When they're ready, take 'em out, pat 'em down one more time with the rub, and place 'em on the grill. Sear the chops by increasin' the surface temperature. They should cook for 3 minutes on both sides, then turn the heat down a bit. Cook for 15 minutes on one side, then 13 minutes on the other. Test the meat temperature. If it gets higher than 155 degrees F., take the chops off at once. You want to reach 145 to 155 degrees F. tops. Once the chops've gotten to the right temperature, take 'em off and place your Velveeta on each one. Let it start to melt, then top it with the salsa.

—Buck N. Hiney, Lot #1

NELLIE TINKLE'S TENDER RIBS

Oh, these will blow a pipe on your organ.

Makes 4 to 6 servin's

4 pounds pork ribs
2 or more cans RC cola
1 pound sawdust
1 batch Kansas City Good Time Rub (pages 157–58)
Your favorite BBQ sauce for bastin'

Cut up your pork ribs and toss 'em in a bakin' dish. Pour the RC cola over the ribs. If it don't cover 'em, add more RC cola till it does. Cover, place in the fridge, and let set for 1½ hours. Take the ribs out of the fridge and place them on a paper towel, and set aside briefly.

Take your sawdust and put it in the RC cola bakin' dish. Set aside.

Grab those ribs and put 'em in a big freezer bag. Add the rub and shake real good. Put the bag and all back in the fridge for another hour.

Take a coffee filter and carefully pour the RC cola through it, strainin' out the sawdust. Place the sawdust on a paper towel. When the hour is up, take the sawdust and sprinkle some of it on the BBQ fire. When it starts to smoke, place your ribs on the medium-low heat and close the lid. Every 30 minutes, go and quickly add more sawdust, then close the lid. Cook for an hour. If the meat thermometer reads 160 degrees F., go ahead and give your ribs a bastin' of your favorite BBQ sauce, toss in any sawdust that you got left, and let 'em cook for another 10 minutes. If it don't read that temperature, then keep cookin' till it does. Once it gets there, then you can add the BBQ sauce. Take off the BBQ and serve.

—Nellie Tinkle, Lot #4

MY BIG FAT GREEK PORK SANDWICH

Lulu Bell saw that Greek movie six times at the Dusty Comet Drive-in and would have watched it a seventh time as well if they hadn't caught her up in that tree. She just loves that there movie.

Makes 4 sandwiches

1 (2-pound) pork loin, boneless
4 tablespoons olive oil
1 tablespoon yellow mustard
½ cup lemon juice
2 cloves garlic, minced
1 teaspoon oregano
1 cup plain yogurt
1 cucumber, very finely chopped
½ teaspoon crushed garlic
½ teaspoon pickle juice
4 pita breads
1 cup red onions, finely chopped

Slice the pork into thin slices, and then cut those slices into strips. Set aside.

In a large bowl, add the olive oil, mustard, lemon juice, minced garlic, and oregano. Mix well. Add the pork strips, makin' sure that they are completely covered. Wrap up and put in the fridge for 6 to 8 hours.

Durin' the last hour, combine the yogurt, cucumber, crushed garlic, and pickle juice. Mix well, cover, and place in the fridge as well.

Take out your pork, drain it, and place it on the grill topper. BBQ for 6 minutes on one side and 4 on the other. It should be a bit crisp. Take it off the BBQ and place it in the pita breads, which you should have cut in halves already. Add the onions followed by the yogurt sauce. Serve with fries.

—*Lulu Bell Boxcar, Lot #8*

DONNA SUE'S PORK RUMP DELIGHT

Oh, this one would be too easy—so I'll just shut my mouth.

Makes 4 to 6 servin's

1 (4-pound) pork shoulder
3½ ounces liquid smoke
6 cups chopped onions
½ cup cider vinegar
2 tablespoons deli mustard
1 tablespoon molasses
¼ teaspoon Tabasco sauce
4 tablespoons Worcestershire sauce
2 cups ketchup
½ cup brown sugar
½ cup chili sauce
½ lemon, sliced
2 teaspoons salt
¼ teaspoon black pepper

Put your pork on a big piece of heavy foil that will cover it completely. Push the foil up a bit so that the pork is still showin' but you can pour your liquids on it without 'em runnin' out of the foil. Add your liquid smoke and 3 cups of the onions. Close the foil up tight and place on your BBQ. Let it cook, fat side up, for 3 hours at 350 degrees F. Turn it over and cook for 3 more hours, makin' sure to open the top of the foil durin' the last 45 minutes. Take it off the grill and make sure that the inside temperature is around 160 degrees F. If it ain't, cook that sucker till it is. When it's done, let it cool down for an hour. Then place it in a pan and wrap it with plastic wrap. Put it in the fridge to set overnight.

In a large bowl, combine all the rest of the ingredients and 1 cup of those juices that should still be in the foil you cooked the pork in. Mix this all together and simmer on the stove for 5 minutes, stirrin' occasionally. Cover and place this in the fridge to set overnight as well.

The next day, take out your sauce that you made the night before and put it in a great big pot. Simmer on low.

Take out your pork and cut off all the fat you can. Pull the meat apart into little shredded sections and put in the pot with the simmerin' sauce. You can also take an electric knife and shred the pork as well. Stir the meaty sauce ever few minutes so none of it sticks to the bottom of the pan. Once it's heated up, transfer it into a big pan and serve. This is great by it-self or on bread.

—Donna Sue Boxcar, Lot #6

Chapter 7

Dick Inman and his wife, Opal Lamb-Inman, of Lot # 1 enjoy a lamb kabob durin' our annual Grape Stompin' Italian Festival and BBQ.

Lamb

In recent years the women of our local chapter of BABL (Baptist Association of Baptized Ladies), in an attempt to show that they respect all nationalities regardless of what their newsletters might say, signed on to join with the traditional town sponsors (the High Chaparral Trailer Park, the Great Big Balls Bowling Alley, and the Pangburn Diner) for the annual Grape Stompin' Italian Festival and BBQ. While the menfolk fire up the BBQ, we ladies dress up like Sophia Loren, well, as close as we can, I should add, and head on over to the high school dunk tank that they set up in front of the trailer park office. Rather than have it filled with water, they load it with grapes. Each one of us gals take our turn settin' on the seat, and people pay a dollar to throw a ball at the target. If they hit it we fall in and have to spend the next few minutes stompin' grapes to the accompaniment of a Tony Bennett or Dean Martin selection. This continues until the grapes are mush or we've run out of fake Sophia Lorens. This year, since they provided the grapes, all the money went to a special fund the ladies of BABL have set up called Money for Needy People with Italian-Soundin' Names Fund. We all have a good time, and of course with the numerous hammer toes, corns, calluses, and bunions that we ladies have from years of wearin' them dang cheap shoes they sell downtown at Sally's Shoe Bonanza, nobody would knowingly drink anything made out of that juice that was in the dunk tank anyways. Rumor has it that before Dora Beaver died, she'd bottle it all up and sell it off as cookin' sherry. Now that Dora's gone we'll never know, but this year since the president of BABL, Dottie Lamb, got the responsibility of disposin' of the stomped juice, we hear she sold it to a convenience store in Conway, Arkansas, for use in their slurpy machine. But now, don't you folks worry, Pastor Ida May Bee said a prayer over it before Dottie hauled it off.

Of course, she also said a prayer over the wonderful BBQ delights that the menfolks created on the BBQ as well. The next best thing to fallin' into a tub of smashed grapes has to be the wonderful BBQin' that goes on. This time of year, in keepin' with the theme, the menfolk tend to add a few of our lamb recipes to the BBQ. Now let me just warn y'all that lamb ain't cheap around these parts, which means the number of recipes are limited, but trust me when I tell y'all, they're pretty doggone tasty. With that said, enjoy what we do got.

KENNY'S BURGUNDY LAMB CHOPS

Leave it to the boys to have a lamb recipe.

Makes 6 servin's

½ cup Burgundy
½ cup olive oil
½ clove garlic, crushed
½ teaspoon salt
½ teaspoon cumin
½ cup chopped red onion
6 lamb chops

Put the first six ingredients in a bowl and whisk them together. Set aside.

Place the lamb chops in a plastic freezer bag and pour the mixed ingredients into the bag. Shake and place in the fridge. Turn the bag over ever 30 minutes for 3 hours. Take the chops out, pat 'em dry with a paper towel, and place 'em on the BBQ. BBQ for 15 minutes on one side, bastin' from time to time, flip the chops, and BBQ for an additional 12 minutes. Boil your marinade and serve with rice or potato salad if rice ain't available at your BBQ.

—*Kenny Lynn, Lot #15*

ZORBA THE BURGER

If this don't make you feel like dancin' with a hanky, nothin' will.

Makes 4 burgers

1 pound ground lamb
2 teaspoons garlic salt
1 tablespoon Dijon mustard
1 tablespoon lemon juice
1 tablespoon minced onion
¼ teaspoon salt
½ teaspoon dried rosemary, crushed
¼ teaspoon pepper
4 hamburger buns
2 tablespoons of your favorite cucumber sauce

Mix the first eight ingredients together in a bowl. Form into 4 patties and cook on the BBQ to your likeness. Serve on the buns and top with cucumber sauce.

—Dottie Lamb, Lot #14

DICK INMAN'S LAMB LOINS

Dick assures me that this is the only lamb loin he'll eat. He is awfully picky.

Makes 4 servin's

1 batch Opal's Lamb Juice (page 153)
8 lamb loin chops

Pour the lamb juice in a big plastic freezer bag, then add the chops. Shake real good and put in the fridge. Let set for 10 minutes, then turn over. Leave for an additional 10 minutes. Take it out of the fridge, drain off the juice into a pan, and place the chops on your BBQ. Baste the chops with the juice in the pan and close the lid. Let 'em cook for about 7 minutes, baste again, and flip each chop. Baste and close the lid. Let 'em cook for around 5 more minutes. Flip the chops again and check the temperature. Your meat thermometer should read 140 to 150 degrees F. for medium rare, 160 degrees F. for medium, and 165 degrees F. or higher for well done. If they ain't done to your likeness, then baste 'em again and let 'em cook for another 5 minutes. Check the temperature. It should be where you want it. You can boil the rest of the lamb juice for 5 minutes to kill the germs from the uncooked meat and use it as a sauce with your chops if you'd like.

—Dick Inman, Lot #1

Chapter 8

There she is: a past Miss Congeniality at one of our annual Little Miss Red, White, and Blue Poultry Pieces contests. Her name slips my mind right off the bat, but her hauntin' aroma still lingers there from time to time.

Chicken

Nothin' says, "God Bless America" like a big old BBQ. A nicely BBQ'd chicken leg is somethin' that most chicken-eatin' Americans hold near and dear to their hearts. So once a year in August we hold a pageant that is open to anyone in the surroundin' area that's under three feet tall and wants to enter, regardless if they live in the park or not. We call it the Little Miss Red, White, and Blue Poultry Pieces contest. And as you can guess, we light up the BBQs for this all-day competition. You should see all the little ones that come to compete. It really is quite cute. The first category is Mystery Marinade Makin', where the contestants have to soak their chicken in a marinade that they've created from two ingredients, which they've randomly selected out of a list of five mystery items. They can add whatever third element they want. I don't think any of us will forget the little gal whose marinade consisted of lemon juice, which she'd brung with her, and the two mystery ingredients that she'd blindly chosen, gunpowder and Everclear. Oh, I tell you, three days later they were still findin' pieces of chicken as far over as Searcy County. Of course, that whole thing made her a shoo-in for Miss Congeniality.

The second event is Creative Chicken Wear, where the contestants come out dressed as their favorite piece of poultry. They can add whatever they'd like to make that piece of chicken their own. Last year Bonita Hix came dressed as a thigh with dyed red, white, and blue hair. She won that section of the contest hands down, but God love her, her poor hair stayed that colored all the way up to Veterans Day, which, come to think of it, was in keepin' with the patriotic theme of the day anyhow. And the sad thing was that Little Bonita was beat out by a sock puppet that Kenny Lynn entered. She had that pageant wrapped up until the talent competition, when the sock puppet whistled "Dixie" while cookin' a split breast. For a piece of woven cotton, that thing could make a mean BBQ'd piece of fowl.

DR PEPPER BBQ CHICKEN

My husband, Dew, will actually put down his fishin' pole for a piece of this.

Makes 4 to 6 servin's

1 cup ketchup
1 can Dr Pepper
1 teaspoon minced garlic
1 teaspoon cayenne pepper
1 teaspoon dry mustard
1 cut-up chicken, washed

Mix the first five ingredients together and pour either into a large skillet or divide into 2 big rectangular cake pans. Regardless of what you put 'em in, put it on the grill. Add your chicken in a single layer. Let cook for 45 minutes to 1 hour, or until the chicken pieces are no longer pink in the middle. Make sure you turn 'em every 15 minutes. If you don't like all the parts of a chicken, feel free to make it all breast or all legs or whatever will make your people happy.

—Mickey Ray Kay, Lot #13

DONNA SUE'S CHICKEN STRIPS

No, this ain't a new act down at the Blue Whale Strip Club.

Makes 8 servin's

8 boneless chicken breast fillets, cut into ¼-inch strips
1 batch Any Old Meat Will Do Rub (page 159)
½ cup Bourbon Street BBQ Sauce (page 145)

Kick your BBQ up to where it's between medium and medium hot. Put your chicken strips into a big bowl and sprinkle on the rub. As you take each strip out of the bowl and place it on the BBQ, make sure that you give it an extra little rub down with the loose excess rub from the bowl. The chicken strips are goin' to grab hold of the grill at first, but if you got your fire hot enough, once they've browned on one side, they'll let go of the grill so you can turn 'em over on the other side. As the strips cook, baste 'em with the sauce. Chicken is cooked when a thermometer reads 165 degrees F.

—*Donna Sue Boxcar, Lot #6*

DOTTIE LAMB'S GRILLED LEMON CHICKEN BREASTS

Believe it or not, she don't sell this at the Superstore.

Makes four servin's

4 chicken breasts, split
1 batch Dottie's Marinade (page 151)

Let your chicken breasts marinate for 1 ½ hours. Take 'em out and place on the BBQ, bone side down first. Let 'em cook for 10 minutes, take 'em off the BBQ, dip back in the marinade, and place back on the grill, bone side up. Let 'em cook for 8 minutes and then flip 'em once more. Let 'em cook for about 3 minutes on the bone side again just to kill the bacteria from the marinade. Put your thermometer in the thickest part of a breast and if it reads 165 degrees F., then they're ready for eatin'.

—*Dottie Lamb, Lot #14*

CHICKEN EL LOIS

Now they got this at the Taco Tackle Shack North, and Lois assures me that by next year they'll start servin' it at the original Taco Tackle Shack, which is located one block down the street. I'm sure all those folks who eat at the latter will sure be glad when this treat sensation finally arrives in their part of town.

Makes 4 servin's

4 skinless chicken breasts
2 tablespoons Crisco, melted
½ cup Taco Tackle Shack's El Rubo (page 000)
1½ cups Velveeta cheese, shredded

½ cup your favorite salsa

4 tablespoons sour cream

Coat your breasts in Crisco. Sprinkle on the rub. Cook on the BBQ at medium-low to medium heat. When they're done, sprinkle the cheese on the chicken breasts, and let melt. Take off the BBQ and put on plates. Spoon onto each chicken breast salsa and 1 tablespoon of sour cream. Serve with hot sauce if desired.

—Lois Bunch, Lot #3

DR PEPPER CAN CHICKEN

Dick also calls this the Happy Chicken. I guess he thinks the chicken likes Dr Pepper.

Makes 1 chicken

1 can Dr Pepper

3 tablespoons apple cider

3 tablespoons Rub My Chicken (page 158)

1 cup Dr Pepper BBQ Sauce (page 135)

1 chicken, cleaned all up and ready for cookin'

The first thing you're goin' to do is get your BBQ up to about 350 degrees F. and put a roastin' pan on the grill. Next you open that can of Dr Pepper and drink half of it. Then you're goin' to add the apple cider to the can. Next you will take one of them can openers like you use when you open a can of tomato juice or such and puncture a few additional holes in the top of that Dr Pepper can. This will give a big enough openin' for the steam to rise from that can when it cooks on the grill. Set the can aside for the time bein'.

Sprinkle about a teaspoon of the rub on the inside of the chicken. Take the remainin' rub and do the outside of the chicken. Now your chicken is just about ready for the grill. Your next step is to set the chicken on top of the Dr Pepper can. This is easy and you shouldn't have any problems, but if you do, just lube your chicken up with a little bit of Crisco. Once you got that can up your chicken's behind, carefully carry the whole thing over to the grill and set straight up in the roastin' pan. It should be restin' securely on its can and two legs. Go ahead and close the lid and let it BBQ for 1½ hours. Durin' the last 15 minutes, baste it with the BBQ sauce. The chicken is done when you poke a thermometer in its breast and it reads 180 degrees F. and the juice from the poke runs clear. Be careful takin' the chicken off the BBQ and enjoy.

—*Dick Inman, Lot #1*

CEREAL CHICKEN KILLER

I like to use Captain Crunch and Frosted Flakes, while Lulu Bell enjoys coatin' her chicken with Fruity Pebbles. I try to skip dinner at her house when she serves this dish.

Makes 4 servin's

3 cups cereal, crushed
1 cup flour
1 teaspoon salt
1 cup milk
1 egg
4 boneless chicken breasts
Corn oil or soy oil for cookin'

Take your cereal and put it in a paper sack. Set aside.

Mix your flour and salt in a bowl and then set aside.

In a separate bowl stir up the milk and egg.

Take your clean chicken breasts and dip both sides in the flour mix, then the milk mixture, followed by shakin' 'em in the cereal sack until well coated. Place 'em in a grill wok, which already has an inch of hot oil in it, and cook for 8 minutes on each side, or until the chicken is 165 degrees F. inside.

—*Lulu Bell Boxcar, Lot #8*

Chapter 9

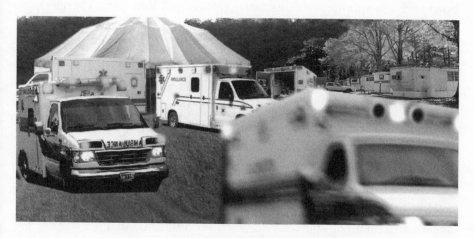

The Veterans Day Fish Fry at the High Chapparal Trailer Park proved once and for all that there's a reason for weight limits.

Fish

Last year, after the town's Veterans Day Parade, we at the High Chaparral Trailer Park threw a fish fry for the town's honorees. We put up the large tent that we'd gotten from Sheriff Gentry. Since he didn't know when he'd have to let those performers from the freak show go, we had to be careful with the tent. The Bunches in Lot #3 provided the fish from the Taco Tackle Shake North since it'd be closed for the holiday.

With Nellie havin' a blister on her finger and couldn't play the organ, Donna Sue was put in charge of providin' the day's entertainment. She had patriotic music playin' over the park's PA system, which along with the good food and conversation, made the day even more special for the vets. Of course that was before three P.M. had rolled around.

No one had noticed that Momma Ballzak had been refillin' the punch bowl ever ten minutes with one part punch and four parts Everclear. So when three P.M. hit and Donna Sue announced it was time for "best dang talent this side of the Mississippi," no one was in the shape to object. Even the unusually quiet Sister Bertha, who'd been fannin' herself as she sipped on her glass of punch, only gave a big smile after the announcement.

"You're a Grand Old Flag" came blarin' over the speakers, and Little Linda, in a two-piece flag-print bathin' suit, came waddlin' into the tent. She went over to Ben Beaver's ridin' lawn mower trailer and crawled onto it, bumpin' and grindin' all 412 pounds to the cheers of the vets. The way their faces lit up, you'd have thought they were children and Santa Claus had just entered the room with candy and toys. They were pullin' out dollar bills and their coin purses, and when she'd finished that gal had money and loose change stickin' out of her bathin' suit as well as every flab of fat that hangs on her body. Well, the show continued with all the Blue Whale girls doin' their part to spread a little joy to the veterans. At the very end, in honor of all the gals who'd served their country with pride and devotion, out came all 358 pounds of exotic male dancer Vance Poole, aka assistant mortician Vance Pool (he adds the *e* to his name when he performs). Before you could say "Where's the beef," Little Linda had come back out and crawled onto the stage with Vance. All that flesh movin' and shakin' was something to see as they danced their exotic ways to everybody's favorite, "Don't Rock the Boat."

"Move over, and let Momma show you how it's done," a familiar voice from the back of the tent yelled out. It was our very own Sister Bertha, who surprisingly had already started removin' items of her clothin'. By the time she'd gotten up on the trailer with the dancers, she'd stripped down to nothin' but her all-in-one girdle! Luckily, for all of us in the tent that day, before she could really start shakin' her groove thing, the lawn mower trailer gave way under all that weight, causin' the three of 'em to come crashin' down onto the whole first row of veterans. With almost 1,100 pounds droppin' from three feet in the air, we knew we'd need an ambulance even before the dust had settled. Nine folks were injured that afternoon with two of 'em havin' to have steel rods implanted in portions of their bodies. One poor man will never regain the sight in his left eye; however, I'm not sure if that specific injury happened before or after the trailer gave way. As luck would have it, neither Sister Bertha nor Little Linda or Vance were hurt. And of course, Sister Bertha ran a full-page ad in the *Bugle* blamin' her behavior on a wonderin' rogue group of Mormons, Jehovah's Witnesses, and atheists who drugged her punch with some kind of non-Christian substance. Regardless, next Veterans Day, blister or not, Nellie Tinkle will be in charge of the celebration's entertainment.

Now, let me just add that even though I don't eat fish unless it comes from Long John Silver, all of the followin' recipes are great. The way I know this is on account of how fast folks that do like fish eat 'em up at our BBQ parties. Also, you must clean and gut all the fish before usin' 'em in these recipes. Duh.

LEMON BUTTER TROUT

I'm sure if I ate fish I'd just love this.

Makes 4 trout

4 trout
¼ cup margarine
2 tablespoons lemon juice
½ teaspoon chervil
¼ teaspoon tarragon

Place your trout on the BBQ and grill for 5 to 6 minutes. Flip 'em, and BBQ 'em for another 5 to 6 minutes on that side as well.

While your fish is cookin' heat the remainin' ingredients in the grill wok on the BBQ grill. Stir well. When you take the fish off the BBQ, spoon a good helpin' of this on 'em and serve.

—*Hubert Bunch, Lot #3*

THE DEVIL'S PET

This fish is so hot, you'll swear they caught it right out of the river Styx.

Makes 4 servin's

4 fish, anything but mackerel
1 cup margarine, melted
2 tablespoons curry powder
1 teaspoon hot sauce
4 hot peppers

Put the fish on the BBQ and grill for 5 minutes on each side. After they're done, take off the grill and slice 'em from front to back so that they spread open. Set aside.

Combine the melted margarine with the curry powder and hot sauce. Stir well. Spread the mixture on the inside and outside of each fish and serve each with a hot pepper.

—*Brother Woody Bee, Lot #7*

DEW'S SIMPLE-AS-CAN-BE TROUT RECIPE

Not only is this simple, but Lulu Bell loves it as well.

Makes 4 trout

4 trout, cleaned, gutted, and deheaded
1 cup Any Old Meat Will Do Rub (page 159)
1 cup diced onions
½ cup margarine

Take each trout and rub it down with the rub. Sprinkle a little inside the body of the fish as well. PLace ¼ cup of the onions and 2 tablespoons of the margarine inside the body of each fish. Wrap 'em in foil and cook for 8 minutes on one side and 7 minutes on the other.

—*Dew Ballzak, Lot #18*

DONNA SUE'S SIMPLE-AS-CAN-BE DRUNKEN TROUT RECIPE

Yes, this is the same recipe as my husband, Dew's, but with my sister's special touch.

Makes 4 happy trout

4 trout, cleaned, gutted, and deheaded
1 cup beer
1 cup Any Old Meat Will Do Rub (page 159)
1 cup diced onion
½ cup margarine

Take each trout and rub it down with a coatin' of beer, followed by a rub-down of the rub. Sprinkle a little inside the body of the fish as well. Place ¼ cup of the onions, 2 tablespoons of the margarine, and ¼ of whatever is left of the beer inside the body of each fish. Wrap in foil and cook for 8 minutes on one side and 7 minutes on the other.

—*Donna Sue Boxcar, Lot #6*

MOMMA BALLZAK'S SIMPLE-AS-CAN-BE TROUT RECIPE

Even my husband, Dew's own momma has to take his recipe and distort it.

Makes 4 trout

4 trout, cleaned, gutted, and deheaded
1 cup vodka
1 cup Any Old Meat Will Do Rub (page 159)
½ cup diced onions
½ cup finely chopped celery
1 cup tomato juice

Take each trout and rub it down with a coatin' of vodka, followed by a rubdown of the rub. Sprinkle a little inside the body of the fish as well. Mix the onions and celery together in a bowl. Add the remainin' vodka and tomato juice to the bowl. Mix well. Divide this into 4 portions. Place 1 portion inside the body of each fish. Wrap in foil and cook for 8 minutes on one side and 7 minutes on the other.

—*Momma Ballzak, Lot #16*

FAYE FAYE LARUES'S BETTER THAN DONNA SUE'S SIMPLE-AS-CAN-BE DRUNKEN TROUT RECIPE

As you can plainly see, the rivalry is still goin' strong.

Makes 4 happy trout

4 trout, cleaned, gutted, and deheaded
1 cup red wine
1 cup Any Old Meat Will Do Rub (page 159)
1 cup diced onion
½ cup margarine
½ cup grated Parmesan cheese

Take each trout and rub it down with a coatin' of red wine, followed by a rubdown of the rub. Sprinkle a little rub inside the body of the fish as well. Place ¼ cup of the onions, 2 tablespoons of the margarine, ¼ of whatever is left of the red wine, and 2 tablespoons of the Parmesan cheese inside the body of each fish. Wrap in foil and cook for 8 minutes on one side and 7 minutes on the other.

—Faye Faye Larue, Lot #17

VANCE POOL'S PORK ENTOMBED TROUT

I have no idea where he came up with this name, but I will tell you that if he's comin' over to eat, you better add another eight trout.

Makes 4 trout

4 trout, cleaned and gutted
16 slices bacon
1 lemon, sliced into 4 wedges

Take a trout and wrap it up with 4 slices of bacon, usin' wooden toothpicks, which you've presoaked in water, to hold the bacon on. BBQ the trout on one side until the bacon slices are cooked, or about 5 minutes each, then flip. Take off the BBQ. Remove the toothpicks and squeeze a lemon wedge over each trout.

—Vance Pool, Lot #19

Chapter 10

No matter how many times I see this photo of Wendy Bottom of Lot #4, it still makes me hungry for a big ol' mouth-waterin' kabob and a box of Godiva chocolates.

Kabobs

I just love kabobs! Not only are they good tastin', but with all the fun food items you can put on a skewer, they can really add a lot of color to a BBQ. As a matter of fact, we folks at the High Chaparral make kabobs the first thing we BBQ come May. That's right, we hold a May Day BBQ each year. Now I know some of y'all are askin' what is so special about May that would have a whole trailer park excited enough to cook out. Well, the answer is simple. Come May the weather is good enough that we can finally take the insulation off our grills and pack it away until the weather turns cold again in November or December. So we mark this day by grillin' up kabobs on our unwrapped BBQs and dancin' around a makeshift maypole that we make by attachin' some long strings of ribbon to the electrical pole that sets out by the office. We had a great time doin' this until last year when we almost got electrocuted. All them sparks and that loud cracklin' liked to scared most of us out of our britches. So this last year we decided to do away with the highly dangerous maypole and simply opt for the kabob cookin' and a Lady Godiva Parade instead.

I'm sure y'all know the story of Lady Godiva and how she rode around town naked on a white horse so that her husband would lower the taxes on the townspeople. Well, since the ride took place in May, we decided to honor this fair maid by doin' our own ride while the kabobs were cookin' durin' the May Day BBQ. We knew it wouldn't lower our taxes, but what the heck, it couldn't hurt, if you know what I mean. So, all the gals who wanted to partake threw their names in a hat, and the one that was drawn would be our Queen of the Kabobs as well as the official Lady Godiva. Well, as luck would have it, our very first Queen of the Kabobs/Lady

Godiva was none other than dear old Wendy Bottom. Needless to say, it made her day. And just as soon as the mail had arrived, Ben Beaver put the chain on the trailer park entrance so no one would come in and interrupt Wendy's royal ride in the buff. Now, we didn't have a white horse for Wendy to ride, but Ben was happy to volunteer the park's white ridin' lawn mower. So after a few minutes of instructions on how to make the mower move and stop, Wendy was just about ready for her maiden journey around the park. I made sure that the long blonde wig she was wearin' was securely bobby-pinned to her head. Since that was the only thing coverin' up her adult sections, we all most assuredly wanted to make sure it stayed on. Well, Ben fired up the lawn mower and we all went into our trailers, leavin' our kabobs cookin' on the BBQ, and Wendy to disrobe and mount the noisy sputterin' white mechanical beast. That thing was so loud when she took off we could hear it clear up in our trailers. Of course I can honestly say that none of us were peekin' out our windows while this bare-butt-naked eighty-nine-year-old gal with a crutch rode around the trailer park. But maybe we should have. If we'd been peepin', we'd have noticed she was in trouble a lot sooner. Somehow the hair from the wig got caught up in the back wheels of the mower, which in turn began to slowly pull her unclothed little wrinkled body back in the seat. Unfortunately, we didn't hear her frantic cries of help until after she'd managed to shut the thing off by bangin' the ignition switch with her cane. By then she was spread-eagle across the back of the mower tryin' in vain to get the tangled wig off her head. Everybody in the trailer park came runnin' out to help. By the time we got that wig unpinned and off her head she was in pieces. Poor Wendy had been through hell. It was terrible seein' her yellin' like that. To be honest, it was really terrible seein' her naked. I'll never be able to look at a prune the same way. Needless to say, Wendy had to lay down and try to recover from that horrific experience. Still, she was able to eat about three kabobs before retirin' into Lot #3.

Did I mention that next year we'll be goin' back to the electric pole thing for the trailer park May Day BBQ?

BILLY BOB'S KABOBS

Lulu Bell says that next to playin' with his hose, eatin' these are Billy Bob's favorite things to do.

Makes 3 good-size kabobs

1 regular can Spam, cut into 1-inch cubes
1 onion, cut into chunks
1 green bell pepper, cut into chunks
1 red bell pepper, cut into chunks
Your favorite BBQ sauce

Place the items in this order on the skewers: Spam, onion, green bell pepper, onion, red bell pepper, onion. Repeat this order until the skewers are full. Give 'em a nice coat of your favorite BBQ sauce and place on BBQ. Let each side cook for 5 minutes, bastin' the kabob with the BBQ sauce constantly.

—*Lulu Bell Boxcar, Lot #8*

PIG AND A PICKLE KABOBS

These are pretty doggone tasty when you consider they come from a gal whose momma's a slut.

Makes about 8 kabobs

1 regular bottle maple syrup
⅓ cup yellow mustard
1½ pounds ham, cut into 1-inch pieces
1 regular jar sweet pickles
1 regular can peaches, halved and cut into bite-size chunks

Put the syrup, mustard, and ham in a big bowl and stir. Place in the microwave for 4 minutes on high. Stir and let it cook another 5 minutes on medium. Add the pickles and peaches and cook for 3 more minutes on medium. Place a piece of ham on a skewer followed by a pickle and a peach chunk. Repeat. BBQ each side 3 minutes for about 30 minutes total all together. Just make sure you keep brushin' your kabobs.

—Tina Faye Stopenblotter, Lot #17

THE VERY TASTY SHISH KABEN

I think this is some kind of code between Dottie Lamb and Ben Beaver. I got a feelin' she's doin' more than just BBQin' his meat for him, but don't quote me on that.

Makes 8 good-size kabens

1 pound sirloin steak, cut into 1½-inch cubes
1 large green bell pepper, cut into 1-inch pieces
2 medium yellow onions, quartered
2 medium-size tomatoes, quartered
½ cup lemon juice
¼ cup soy sauce
1 tablespoon Worcestershire sauce
1 teaspoon yellow mustard

Place your steak, green bell pepper, onions, and tomatoes in a bowl and add your lemon juice, soy sauce, Worcestershire sauce, and mustard. Swish everything around and let it set for 2 hours in the fridge. Skewer the items in the bowl startin' with the meat then onion, green bell pepper, and tomato. Repeat and place on the BBQ for 7 minutes on each side. Brush on the mixture in the bowl from time to time up until just before you make the last turn. If you need to cook it longer to get a more well done-ness to the meat, do so, but don't use the marinade for the last 7 minutes. It ain't healthy.

—Dottie Lamb, Lot #14

LULU BELL'S SHISH KABOOMS

God bless her, she does try.

Makes 8 to 10 servin's

½ cup soy sauce
½ cup Tabasco sauce
3 tablespoons honey
2 tablespoons vinegar
1 tablespoon cayenne pepper
1½ teaspoons garlic powder
½ teaspoons powdered ginger
¾ cup vegetable oil
1 green onion, finely chopped
2½ pounds boneless beef sirloin, cut into 1½-inch cubes
1 (8-ounce) can pineapple chunks, drained
2 red onions, cut into 1½-inch wedges
3 green bell peppers, cut into 1½-inch chunks
1 pound Polish sausage links, cut into 1½-inch cubes

Combine the first nine ingredients together in a bowl. Mix well. Add only the beef and cover. Place it in the fridge and let it set over night. Take out the beef and pat it dry. Place the items in this order on the skewers: beef, pineapple, onion, green bell pepper, sausage, onion, pineapple, green bell pepper, and repeat. Brush the items with the marinade and BBQ each side for 5 minutes, brushin' the marinade often. Stop marinadin' and instead pour the marinade in a pan or skillet and set it directly on the grill. BBQ your meat 1 more minute on each side while you bring the marinade in the pan to a boil. Take the kabooms off the BBQ. Let the marinade boil for 5 minutes. Take it off the grill and serve it as sauce with the kabooms.

—Lulu Bell Boxcar, Lot #8

BEN BEAVER'S TROUT KABOBS

I tell y'all, you ain't seen a man who'll fight a fish on a line as hard as old Ben Beaver will. Of course, if you go with him to fish on his pontoon boat, remind him to lock the wheels on his wheelchair or both you and him are gonna spend some time in the water.

Makes 6 to 8 skewers' worth

4 trout, cleaned, gutted, and with the head and tail cut off
1 batch of Beaver Rub (page 160)
2 bakin' potatoes, cut into ½-inch cubes
1 onion, cut into bite-size pieces
1 cup vegetable oil
2 lemons, cut into wedges

Take your trout and cut 'em up into 3-inch-long pieces. Rub these pieces with the rub. Set aside the remainin' rub.

Put the trout sections and the veggies on the skewers, alternatin' in any order. Place 'em on the BBQ. Add the rub to the oil, stir well, and brush on the cookin' trout and veggies. BBQ on each side for 4 minutes. You can cook longer just as long as you keep the trout well oiled, or if it's done before the veggies, then just take 'em all off the skewers, put the veggies together in a skillet with the rub oil mixture, and fry up on the BBQ. Pour this entire mixture over the trout pieces and serve. Squeeze lemon wedges over the servin's.

—*Ben Beaver, Lot #14*

LOVIE BIRCH'S FUND-RAISER KABOBS

Many a democratic hopeful has got their campaign money, thanks to these little sticks of meat.

Makes 6 servin's

1 pound sirloin, cut into 1-inch cubes
2 bunches green onions, white part only
28 cherry tomatoes

2 dozen mushrooms (the ones from the store)
1 yellow bell pepper, cut into pieces
1 red bell pepper, cut into pieces
1 green bell pepper, cut into pieces

Place a piece of each item on skewers in any order you'd like. BBQ for 5 minutes on each side.

—Lovie Birch, Lot #20

TRAILER PARK KABOBS

Now you're talkin'!

Makes 4 kabobs

2 pounds hamburger meat
2 cups hamburger pickle slices
1 onion, cut into chunks
1 green bell pepper, cut into chunks
1 pound Polish sausage, cut into 1-inch pieces

Roll your raw hamburger meat into golf ball–size balls. With your hand around your ball for support, carefully slide it on a skewer, all the way to the bottom. Next add a pickle, an onion, a pickle, a green bell pepper, a pickle, an onion, a pickle, a piece of sausage, a pickle, a green bell pepper, a pickle, an onion, and a pickle. Repeat until your skewer is full, then do the rest in the same manner. Coat this with a BBQ sauce (any of the ones in Chapter 15 will work) and BBQ for 3 minutes on each side for about 30 minutes. Make sure you put sauce on each side before and after you turn the skewer. Serve with bread.

—Ruby Ann Boxcar, Lot 18

Chapter 11

Nellie Tinkle admires this veteran's sausage at the VFW Memorial Day BBQ.

Sausages

Every Memorial Day we hold German Night at the VFW to raise money for needy veterans. Those pants that go all the way up to your chest seem to cost more and more each year. Of course in honor of this special night, we prepare the fellas some real good German food like German Potato Salad, German Spinach, and of course BBQ'd German Sausage Links. It just makes the fellas real happy and all. And then around five P.M., after the wonderful German food, there's always the dance portion of the night. My sister's group, Donna Sue Boxcar and Her One-Night Stands, always volunteer to play the dance music for the men and women who served our country. And I take the vocals. I don't know who has more fun, us up onstage or the folks dancin'. Needless to say, a good time is had by all. Of course, since most of these dear sweet vets are pooped out after one or two polkas, the whole thing's usually over by five-thirty, which is nice 'cause we usually lose the ones that don't dance so they can get home in time for *Wheel of Fortune*. Since we ain't got a lot of vets left from the WWII era, there's been talk about maybe changin' the event over to Korean food instead. Lord, I hope not. I don't know any Korean songs.

KELLY RIPA'S TRIBUTE HOT LINKS

Lulu Bell says these are as hot as Kelly and her husband on All My Children.

Makes as many hot links as there are in your package

1 package hot links
2 tablespoons chili powder

2 tablespoons brown sugar
1 tablespoon cayenne pepper
1 cup hot sauce
1 can beer

Open the package of hot links and cut them in half lengthways. Set aside.

Mix the next three ingredients. Once they are mixed well, add the hot sauce. Mix well with an electric mixer. Add the beer. Mix. Add the hot links, cover, and place in the fridge for 1 hour. Take the links out and place 'em on the BBQ and let 'em cook for about 3 minutes on each side. Cook 'em until you get the your desired doneness. Serve.

—Lulu Bell Boxcar, Lot #8

GERMAN SAUSAGE

These are also known the world over as bratwurst, but since none of us at the High Chaparral Trailer Park are bisexual and have problems pronouncin' them foreign words, let alone English, we just call 'em German sausages.

Makes 4 servin's

2 cans beer
1 onion, diced
1 can sauerkraut
2 tablespoons garlic salt
⅛ teaspoon cumin
1 package bratwurst

Mix the beer, onion, sauerkraut, garlic salt, and cumin together. Place the mixture in a pan and put it on the BBQ. Once it starts to boil, add your bratwurst. Let 'em cook for 10 minutes. Next put your grill wok on the BBQ and transfer your bratwurst, onion, and sauerkraut from the pan to the grill wok. Let cook, turnin' everythin' until it gets nice and brown on the outside. Then dip it back in the pan of boilin' beer and onto a plate.

—Wendy Bottom, Lot #4

HARLAND'S SHRIVELED WIENIE BAKE

This is real good with them old wienies that you have left over from BBQin'.

Serves 4 to 6

2 boxes macaroni and cheese
4 to 6 leftover BBQ'd wienies, chopped into bite-size pieces
6 cherry tomatoes, cut into quarters
2 cups Velveeta cheese, shredded

Make the macaroni and cheese accordin' to the box. Add the wienies and cherry tomatoes. Stir well. Place in a bakin' dish and cover with the cheese. Bake in the microwave until the cheese melts. Take out and stir.

—Harland Hix, Lot #9

Chapter 12

You can tell just by lookin' at this old photo that it was taken at one our
Washington's Birthday BBQs on account of the fact that my late Pa-Pa is all
dressed up in his George Washington outfits and one of Great Aunt Leela's wigs.
That bread he's got under his arm is his infamous cherry bread, which it looks
like he'd already sunk them wooden teeth into. Oh, how I miss that old man.

Breads

My dear departed Pa-Pa used to make a bread every year for the trailer park's George Washington's Birthday BBQ, that was really somethin' to taste. It was his Cherry Bread Surprise, and we used to wait with anticipation around the High Chaparral for our first president's birthday to fall just because of this bread. Oh sure, we loved all the other wonderful cherry dishes that the gals at the trailer park used to make in honor of this special day, but there was nothin' like Pa-Pa's bread. We all think that one of the reasons it was so dang good was 'cause of his love for George Washington. For Pa-Pa, President Washington was a hero to look up to as well as try to emulate. And trust me when I say that on George's birthday, Pa-Pa took that emulatin' part way past the limit of normal human behavior; I'm not just talkin' about the Pa-Pa's Favorite Cherry Bread Surprise.

Pa-Pa, who was a very patriotic man, carved out a set of wooden teeth back in 1954. Every year on George Washington's birthday he'd take out his good teeth and wear those wooden teeth all day long in honor of our first president. All us kids in the trailer park would get such a kick out it when Pa-Pa would talk to us with those wooden teeth in his mouth. It was one of the funnier things I can recall seein' up until I was old enough to date. Of course it wasn't that fun for Pa-Pa. I can't tell you all the misery he went through on account of those wooden teeth.

One year durin' a flare-up, a wild ember from the BBQ he was mannin' out in my front yard caught his dang wooden choppers on fire. God bless him, his denture adhesive had bonded so tightly with the wood that he couldn't get the burnin' teeth out. Well, luckily we rushed him into my trailer home, grabbed a butter knife, and tried to pry 'em out. As my husband, Dew, did everythin' he could in an attempt to get those flamin' teeth out of Pa-Pa's mouth, he was forced to chatter his blazin' choppers together in an attempt to pound out the flames. It looked like someone had popped a set of them wind-up teeth in his mouth. Finally, once I made it to the kitchen, I turned on the tap and dosed Pa-Pa with the spray hose on my kitchen sink. Pa-Pa was shaken, but fine. My trailer smelt of burnt wood for two weeks, which was nice 'cause the odor made it seem like we had a real fireplace in the livin' room.

Then there was the year later on that he was out on his trailer roof wearin' a new set of them teeth he'd made and tryin' to adjust his antenna when he was attacked by a woodpecker. That was a terrible sight for us little ones to watch. To this day I can't set through a whole Woody Woodpecker cartoon. If only we'd had counselin' back then like they do now, my life might have been different.

Who can forget the Washington's Birthday that Pa-Pa got infested with termites? He was so miserable from them little critters that he didn't even take the time to read the warnin' label printed on the Raid can before he used it. That wasn't pretty either, but Pa-Pa insisted he do his part in rememberin' this great man's birthday. Well, we finally put our foot down three years later when he came down with Dutch elm disease. That was the end of Pa-pa's wooden choppers. Now that I'm older and Pa-Pa has gone on to meet his maker, every year when February 22 arrives, I make up that cherry bread, and wish we'd kept a set of those timber teeth of his even though by the time we finally got him to throw 'em away they had wood rot and smelt like Limburger cheese gone bad.

PA-PA'S FAVORITE CHERRY BREAD SURPRISE

In lovin' memory of Pa-Pa, and George Washington, of course.

Makes 2 loaves

12 ounces cream cheese, softened
3 eggs
4 cups self-risin' flour
2 cups sugar

2 teaspoons bakin' powder

1 teaspoon bakin' soda

1 teaspoon salt

1 teaspoon cinnamon

1½ cups vegetable oil

1 teaspoon vanilla extract

1 can cherry pie fillin'

1½ cups chopped pecans

Beat your cream cheese until it's nice and fluffy, then add 2 of the eggs and beat well. In a new bowl, mix your next 6 ingredients together.

Take the last egg and put it in a container and shake it for 10 seconds. Pour it into the flour bowl, then add the oil and vanilla as well. Stir. Add the cherry pie fillin' and the pecans. Divide the batter into two bowls. Take one bowl and pour half the batter into one loaf pan and the rest into the other loaf pan. Put half your cream cheese mixture on top of the dough in one pan, and the other half in the second pan. Now take your other bowl of dough and put half on top of the cream cheese in the first pan and then do the same to the second pan. Loosely wrap the loaves in foil so that they have enough room to increase in size, and set 'em away from the heat source in a grill that reads 350 degrees F. Close the lid, maintain that temperature, and bake for 1 hour. Test the bread with a toothpick to make sure that it comes out clean. If it don't, bake for another 20 minutes and try again.

—*Momma Boxcar, Lot #5*

ME-MA'S CORN BREAD SECRET

This is a secret she could have taken to her grave. Please don't even attempt this one!

Makes 1 loaf

1 loaf bread

1 can creamed corn

1 can kernel corn

1 cup honey

Mix all together. Put in greased large cake pan. Cook for 20 minutes at 400 degrees F. Serve with a whole onion. Everybody loves my secret corn bread. Remember, it's a secret!

—Me-Ma, Formerly of Lot #16

GARLIC CHEESE BREAD

This is one of the only times Momma don't use Velveeta when she cooks.

Makes 4 to 6 servin's

1 loaf French bread
¼ cup margarine, melted
2 tablespoons olive oil
2 tablespoons garlic powder
1 tablespoon parsley flakes
½ cup Parmesan cheese
1 cup mozzarella cheese

Cut the loaf in half lengthwise.

Mix the margarine, olive oil, garlic powder, and parsley together. Brush it on each half of the loaf. Make sure you use all of it. Add the cheeses. Put the two halves together and wrap in foil. Place on the grill and let it cook for 5 minutes. Turn and let cook for 5 more minutes. Enjoy. Wrap up whatever you don't eat and throw it in the fridge. This is good reheated.

—Momma Boxcar, Lot #5

OLLIE WHITE'S TASTY BUNS

Not only are her buns tasty, but they also feel real good too.

Makes 25 buns

¼ cup yeast
½ cup warm water, 105 to 110 degrees F.
¾ cup water

3 eggs
⅔ cup sugar
3 tablespoons powdered milk
2¼ teaspoons salt
6¼ cups plus 2 tablespoons flour
½ cup shortenin'
Melted margarine for brushin'

Sprinkle the yeast over the ½ cup warm water, which you've put in a mixin' bowl. Stir and set aside for 5 minutes.

In a large bowl, combine the next five ingredients and mix using a dough hook until the ingredients are just mixed. Add the flour and yeast solution. Mix for 1 minute on low, or until all the flour and yeast have mixed into the wet ingredients. Add the shortenin' and mix for another minute on low speed. Kick the mixer up to medium speed and let it rip for another 10 minutes, or until dough is smooth and elastic. Cover and let it set in a warm place for about 1½ hours, or until it doubles in size.

Punch down the dough and take it out of the bowl. Shape in a rectangular shape and let it rest for 20 minutes. Divide the dough into 25 sections and shape each one into a ball by rollin' with a circular motion on the table. Place each ball about 2 inches away from each other on a greased bakin' pan. When the balls have risen to about two thirds larger, flatten each ball with your hand till it's about ½ inch thick. Brush a little margarine on top of each ball and bake 'em at 350 degrees F. for 10 to 15 minutes, or until golden brown. Take 'em out of the oven and brush another coat of margarine on each. Allow to sit for 30 more minutes or until they've cool. Slice each bun across to make a hamburger bun. Store in a plastic bag.

—*Ollie White, Lot #10*

NELLIE TINKLE'S WORLD'S BEST RHUBARB BREAD

Nellie makes this only three times a year—for Mother's Day, our first summer trailer park BBQ, and on the Saturday after Thanksgivin', when she makes two loaves for her and C.M. to munch on and share with others when they go up to watch the Flippin' Merchant's Association Holiday Parade.

Makes 2 loaves

1 cup brown sugar
½ cup sugar
⅔ cup vegetable oil
2 eggs
1 cup milk
1 teaspoon salt
1 teaspoon vanilla extract
2½ cups flour
1½ teaspoons baking powder
½ teaspoon baking soda
2 cups diced rhubarb

Combined all the ingredients in a large bowl and mix well. Divide into two sections of dough and place in greased loaf pans. Cover with foil, leavin' a tent at the top of each one, and BBQ for 1 hour at 350 degrees F.

—*Nellie Tinkle, Lot #4*

ELROY'S GARLIC ROLLS

Leave it to an eighty-year-old exotic male dancer to come up with somethin' this easy to make.

Makes as many as are in the bag

½ cup margarine
1 clove garlic, crushed
1 bag ready-to-serve rolls

Place the margarine and crushed garlic in a metal bowl and set on the BBQ where the heat is low, like over on the front left or right side. After the butter is melted, stir it up real good and let it set there for about 1½ to 2 minutes. Don't let it get browned. Take it off the burner and set it aside.

Take the rolls out of the bag and dip the top of each one into the margarine mixture. Place the rolls, tops up, on a double-layered piece of heavy foil. Wrap the whole thing up good and tight and put on the BBQ. Let it cook for 15 to 20 minutes. Serve hot. You can use the brown-and-serve rolls, but they need 20 to 25 minutes.

—*Elroy Dasafe, Lot #19*

STICK BREAD

Lord, if this don't scream country, I don't know what does!

Makes 8

1 roll refrigerated biscuit dough
8 sticks, cleaned

Pop open your can of biscuits and take out one servin' or a single helpin' of biscuit dough. Stretch the dough out so it's nice and long. Wrap it around the end of a stick, makin' sure that the part at the end of the stick closes tightly around the stick. Now hold over the BBQ and slightly above the grill and cook for 12 to 20 minutes, or until the dough gets a golden brown. Make sure you turn your stick often durin' this cookin' time. When you've finished, carefully slide the cooked biscuit off the stick. You should have a deep hollow hole from where the stick was. Fill it with your favorite spread, butter sauce, or meat for that matter. If you got a big stick, then you should be able to shove a good-size wienie into your hole. Personally I like to push some Spam in my hole and top it off with a bit of cheese.

—*Wendy Bottom, Lot #4*

WHERE'S YOUR PAYCHECK BEER BREAD

Knowin' Kitty, I'm sure there's a story here, but I'm just too afraid to ask.

Makes 1 loaf

3 cups self-risin' flour
1 can beer
2 tablespoons sugar
½ teaspoon salt

Mix it all together real good. Grease up a bread pan and place the dough in it. Cover this with foil, but make sure that you leave enough room at the top for the bread to expand. Place your pan on the BBQ away from the fire. You should have preheated your grill to about 350 degrees F. and only have the charcoal or gas flame goin' on one side of the BBQ. Close the lid and let the dough cook for 40 minutes. Take the lid off and quickly open the foil. Brush some margarine on the top and close the lid. Wait for 10 more minutes, give the bread the toothpick check, and if it comes out clean, then the bread's ready to be pulled off the BBQ.

—*Kitty Chitwood, Lot #11*

LAST SUPPER BREAD

Now I know they had Welch's grape juice back at the Last Supper, but I question Sister Bertha's belief that this included their soda version.

Makes 2 loaves

3 cups wheat flour
1 tablespoon instant yeast
12 ounces Welch's grape soda, warm

Take your flour and yeast and mix 'em up real good. Add your grape soda and stir once more. Do not knead. Divide into 2 loafs, and place in greased bread pans. Let 'em rise. Wrap 'em up in foil with lots of room at the top. Stick in the BBQ and grill away from the direct heat for 20 minutes at 375 degrees F.

—*Sister Bertha, Lot #12*

Chapter 13

Pastor Ida May Bee of Lot #7 stands with authority atop the hay wagon as her husband, Brother Woody Bee, pulls her up to the curch on the tractor right before our newly established Baptist Hayride and BBQ. Of course, some folks still brought a casserole. After, all we don't want to be mistaken for Methodist, God forbid!

Side Dishes and Salads

Pastor Ida May Bee really got us this past October when she announced that for the first time in the history of the then First Baptist Church of Pangburn, we'd be havin' a special seasonal celebration for church members and a guest.

"Yes, brothers and sisters, in honor of the lovely changin' of the leaves and the beautiful fall weather that the good Lord has seen fit to bestow upon us, His humble servants who have worked our butts off this year under His ever watchful eye and great big old guidin' hand are gonna have a hayride and BBQ." Even as Pastor Ida May Bee's words rang through the sacred timbers of the church, folks startin' to smile in glee and show their appreciation through applause.

So come the sixth of October, we all met at the front steps of the church dressed in our everyday clothes. And right at 2:30 P.M. sharp Brother Woody Bee came around the corner drivin' a tractor that pulled the hay-covered wagon with Pastor Ida May Bee ridin' on top one of the bales. Why, the way she was smilin' and wavin' at all of us in the cheerin' church crowd, you'd have thought *she* was the new Cow Queen. That election had actually been held just the night before over in Bald Knob, and to everyone's disappointment, Little Linda did not go home with the crown, but she did leave with one of the judges). When that great big old hay wagon came to a stop, we picked up the two grills that me and my husband, Dew, and Dottie Lamb had provided. And then all 126 members that were able to come and their guests climbed aboard with their side dishes and salads. Pastor Ida May Bee had gotten permission to use Old Man Dankin's pasture for the BBQ. It was really pretty over there and close to a small pond. As any good Baptist will tell you, you don't conduct any kind of church function without a body of water bein' close by. Of course, with it bein' as cold as it was, I think that even if Pastor Ida May Bee had been able to walk on that pond, folks still would've asked if they could wait until later to get baptized, but you still got to be prepared. Anyways, with everyone and their food item aboard, Brother Woody Bee kicked that tractor into gear and started off, well, crawlin' on account of the weight. So Pastor Ida May Bee asked all the children and those in their twenties and thirties to please get off and walk alongside the wagon. The tractor was able to pick up speed and it finally started on the five-mile journey to the designated site. Of course, by the time we finally caught up with those on foot, they'd been restin' a quarter of a mile ahead of us. We couldn't just leave 'em there, nor could we take 'em with us. Hungry and mad, Sister Bertha stood up and ordered everyone to drag the hay off and throw it alongside the road. When we'd all got back on the wagon she told Brother Woody to floor it, and sure as a twister in July we started to take off. Twenty minutes later and with four miles still left to go, the decision was made that some of the salads and side dishes would have to be dumped out of their containers and onto the road in order to lighten our load. The first to go, naturally, was the green Jell-O salad. That got rid of 68 out of 140 side dishes right away. You could tell we was suddenly pickin' up more speed, but not enough. Next came anything made with beets or radishes. Another thirteen dishes were tossed to the side. Anything of non-American origin, with baklava and garlic mashed potatoes bein' the exceptions, would be the next winners of our "get it off the wagon" contest. You should've seen the tsatziki and tabouleh flyin', three bowl's worth to be exact. The next items weren't as easy to toss as the ones before had been. The decision was to throw off the coleslaw and potato salad after each one had been sampled. If they were good they'd stay, and if not, well, those would have to go. After a tastin' was held, it was decided that we were goin' fast enough by this time and that Vance Pool's potato salad would be the only item to shake hands with the road (he used mayonnaise instead of Miracle Whip, and it had no mustard in it). Once we finally got there and got the gas BBQs goin', we had a wonderful day. Pastor Ida May Bee preached a terrific sermon, which was really touchin' out there in the beauty and peace of the countryside. Of course, no one was real happy when she announced that there'd be a $2 fee to ride back on the wagon. That was to pay for the meat that the church had provided as well as the rental on the wagon and tractor. What else could we do but pay? Heck, we was five miles out of town. But as we made our journey back we was amazed that most of the food we'd tossed aside durin' our "hayride of the damned" was gone. The little animals in the wilderness had enjoyed a Sunday treat as well. Of course all of Vance Pool's potato salad, even hours later, was still left untouched. Who said animals are dumb? We've decided to make the hayride a yearly event, but we ain't rentin' a tractor to pull our big behinds. No, instead we're checkin' into the rental price on a semitruck. We ain't takin' no more chances.

MOMMA'S GREEN PEA SALAD

My sister used to torment me when I was a little girl by stickin' peas in her nose and shootin' 'em at me. After a while I got to where I could catch 'em with my mouth. I just love peas.

Makes 4 good-size servin's

1 (17-ounce) can green peas, drained
3 eggs, hard-boiled and chopped up
½ cup sweet pickle, chopped
½ cup pimiento, chopped
½ cup mayonnaise
¼ cup Velveeta cheese, shredded
¼ teaspoon celery seeds

Put everythin' in a great big bowl and stir, makin' sure to mix well. Cover and put in the fridge so it can chill.

—*Momma Boxcar, Lot #5*

WENDY BOTTOM'S GREEN PEA SALAD

If this is anythin' like her wonderful baked beans, you'll wish you'd eaten 'em alone. You won't want to share.

Makes 4 to 6 servin's

2 cups peas, cooked
½ cup dairy sour cream
½ cup mayonnaise
4 tablespoons celery, very finally chopped
3 tablespoons pickle juice
3 tablespoons finely chopped onion
5 slices bacon, crisp and crumbled

Add everythin' together and chill. If you like it creamier, add more mayonnaise.

—*Wendy Bottom, Lot #4*

JUANITA'S GRILLED CHICKEN FAJITA SALAD

Now old Juanita gives the Taco Tackle Shack a run for their money with this dish.

Makes 4 to 6 servin's

4 boneless grilled chicken breasts, cut into small strips
6 cups chopped lettuce
1 medium red bell pepper, cut into strips
2 medium green onions, sliced
¼ cup vegetable oil
1½ tablespoons cilantro, chopped
3 tablespoons lime juice
1 tablespoon honey
¾ teaspoon cumin
¼ teaspoon salt
⅛ teaspoon pepper
2 cloves garlic, finely chopped

Take your chicken and place in fridge while you prepare this dish.

Take the next three ingredients and toss 'em together in a bowl. Set aside.

Take the remainin' ingredients, minus the chicken, and put into a bowl. Mix with a mixer on high for 3 minutes, or until everythin' is blended together. Take your chicken strips and put 'em on the salad. Pour the dressin' that you just made on top of this and toss it once more. Store in the fridge till it's time to serve.

—Juanita Hix, Lot #9

WANDA KAY'S QUICK AS A FLASH JELL-O SALAD

Now if she could just learn how to use that dang flash on that camera.

Serves 4 to 6

2 cups cottage cheese
1 large container Cool Whip
1 large box strawberry Jell-O
1 regular can crushed pineapple
1 cup miniature marshmallows
¼ cup chopped pecans.

Mix the first four items in a bowl with a mixer until well blended. Add the marshmallows and pecans and stir those in by hand. Pour into a mold or a servin' dish, cover, and chill for at least 6 good hours.

—Wanda Kay, Lot #13

ICE CREAM SHOP SALAD

This salad is real good, but it made me mad. There ain't one drop of ice cream in the whole thing. If it weren't so good I'd most likely have to sue for fraud.

Makes 4 to 6 servin's

1 (13-ounce) can pineapple chunks or wedges
1 (1-ounce) can mandarin oranges

½ cup maraschino cherries
2½ cups miniature marshmallows
½ cup sour cream
6 bananas, split lengthwise and sliced into 1-inch wedges
¼ cup shredded coconut

In a large bowl, combine the pineapple and its juice, mandarin oranges, maraschino cherries, and marshmallows. Add the sour cream and half the bananas. Toss. Top off with the remainin' bananas, sprinkle with the coconut, cover, and then chill in the fridge for 2 hours.

—*Tina Faye Stopenblotter, Lot #17*

CREAMY LEMON SALAD

This stuff don't last five minutes once it hits the table.

Makes 8 to 10 servin's

6 ounces cream cheese, cut into cubes
1 cup miniature marshmallows
10 ounces Sprite
1 regular box lemon Jell-O
1 (20-ounce) can crushed pineapple
1 cup chopped pecans
1 cup Cool Whip

Take your cream cheese and marshmallows and place 'em in a large bowl. Put 'em in the microwave for 1½ minutes on high. Take out and set aside.

Take your Sprite and pour it into a large bowl. Stick it in the microwave for 3 minutes on high. While this is cookin', take a mixer to the cheese mixture and mix for 1 minute on a medium settin'. Add the hot Sprite and mix for another minute or 2 until it is all melted and mixed into one big mess. Add your Jell-O and mix again until it has completely dissolved. Then add your pineapple and its juice along with the pecans. Mix again for 2 minutes. Put into the fridge and let it cool for about 10 or 15 minutes. Take it out and fold in the Cool Whip. 'Cause it goes so fast, nobody will get a chance to see how beautiful your molded version is if you put it in a servin' dish. Don't waste your time; slap it in a dish, cover it, and stick it in the fridge. I used to garnish it with little marshmallows, but now I just throw it on the table and let the vultures go after it.

—*Anita Biggon, Lot #2*

GREEN JELL-O SALAD

I'm only puttin' this recipe out there so that y'all can suffer just like the rest of us in trailer parks around the world have suffered. This is like the poor man's ambrosia salad.

Makes 6 to 8 servin's

1 regular box lime Jell-O
1 cup miniature marshmallows
1 cup boilin' water
1 cup finely shredded cabbage
1 cup crushed pineapple, well drained
½ cup walnuts, chopped
¾ cup mayonnaise
1 small can evaporated milk, chilled

Put your Jell-O and marshmallows in a bowl and add the boilin' water. Take an electric mixer to it and mix until both dissolve in the water. If they don't totally dissolve after 5 minutes of mixin', put the bowl in the microwave and nuke 'em for 2 more minutes. Then try mixin' 'em again. Next add your cabbage, pineapple, walnuts, and mayonnaise. Mix on high for a minute or so until all is mixed well. Cover and put in the fridge for 15 to 20 minutes, or until it starts to set.

In the meantime, whip up your evaporated milk real good. Then take the Jell-O mixture out of the fridge and fold in your whipped milk. Put it in the bowl you want to serve it in, cover, and chill for another 1 or 2 hours. Don't put it in a that Jell-O mold 'cause this stuff ain't up for that. It'll fall all over you like a drunk uncle at a family reunion.

—*Kitty Chitwood, Lot #11*

DONNY'S FRUITSLAW

Boy, there was almost a fight over this dish at our last BBQ. When Donny set it down on the table, Brother Woody asked him what it was. Well, Donny told him that it was an old family recipe called fruitslaw, and I guess Dick Inman and his butler, Bruce, started snickerin'. And Bruce turned to Brother Woody and made some kind of comment about how Donny sure lived up to his dish's name. Well, before you could stick in a Judy Garland eight-track tape, Kenny had jumped up in Bruce's face, and I swear that if Sister Bertha hadn't yelled for them boys to shut up and sit down 'cause she was tryin' to get by with her side dish, there would've been a knockdown right then and there. And all over a little salad.

Makes 4 to 6 servin's

1 cup pineapple chunks
2 tablespoons pineapple juice
2 cups red cabbage
2 cups green cabbage
½ cup chopped dates
½ cup chopped celery
¼ cup shredded carrots
½ cup mayonnaise
1 tablespoon vinegar
½ teaspoon salt
½ teaspoon sugar

Open the can of pineapple chunks and take out 2 tablespoons of juice. Set to the side.

In a large bowl, mix the next six ingredients together. Set aside.

In a separate bowl, combine the remainin' ingredients, includin' the pineapple juice that you put to the side earlier. Pour this dressin' over the items in the large bowl and toss. Put in the fridge to chill and serve.

—*Donny Owens, Lot #15*

FOUR-BEAN SALAD

Yes, you read it right, it ain't three-bean salad, but rather four-bean salad. You know, I love Dottie to death, but sometimes she can be so uppity.

Makes 4 to 6 servin's

1 regular can wax beans, drained
1 regular can green beans, drained
1 regular can kidney beans, drained
1 regular can garbanzo beans, drained
1 red onion, thinly sliced
1 red bell pepper, finely chopped
1 green bell pepper, finely chopped
2 tablespoons soy sauce
¾ cup sugar
1 teaspoon black pepper
½ cup cider vinegar
½ cup vegetable oil

Combine your beans, onion, red bell pepper, green bell pepper, soy sauce, sugar, and black pepper. Pour your last two ingredients over the top of this. Lightly toss, cover, and put in the fridge to chill overnight. Before you take to the BBQ, drain off the juices.

—*Dottie Lamb, Lot #14*

TINA FAYE'S TEMPTIN' TATERS

Instead of gettin' a mint on your pillow after your bed has been turned down at the R.U. Inn, you find a bowl of these.

Makes 6 to 8 servin's

4 baked potatoes, peeled and cubed
4 cloves garlic
2 tablespoons plus ⅛ teaspoon salt

Water for boilin'
¾ cup milk
1 tablespoon olive oil
3 tablespoons margarine, melted
⅛ teaspoon pepper

Place the potatoes, garlic, and 2 tablespoons salt in a pot and add water until they are covered. Bring to a boil. Reduce the heat and let simmer for 10 minutes, covered. Stir with a spoon. Heat up the milk in the microwave and set aside.

Mash the potatoes and add the milk, olive oil, and margarine. Beat till fluffy. Add the ⅛ teaspoon salt and pepper.

—Tina Faye Stopenblotter, Lot #17

HARRY'S BAKED BEAN SALAD

These ain't half bad for a sixty-four-year-old man who mows his yard in a muscle shirt and a thong.

Makes 6 to 8 servin's

4½ cups baked beans, cold
6 slices bacon, cooked crisp and crumbled into tiny bits
¾ teaspoon salt
½ cup olive oil
¾ teaspoon paprika
2 tablespoons vinegar
2 tablespoons chives, finely chopped
3 cups shredded lettuce

Mix all the ingredients together for 2 minutes with a big spoon or spatula. Serve cold.

—Harry Lombardi, Lot #19

MOMMA BALLZAK'S DANCIN' POTATOES

If these don't cook long enough, you'll be dancin' too.

Makes 4 to 6 servin's

6 onions
8 potatoes, peeled
1 tablespoon salt
½ cup margarine, melted
2 cups Tennessee whiskey
½ cup water
4 cups Cheddar cheese

Dice your up your onions and cube your potatoes. Dump 'em in a roastin' pan. Salt 'em.

In a bowl, mix the melted margarine, whiskey, and the water together. Pour that over the onions and potatoes. Add the cheese and mix it all up with the other ingredients. Put in the oven and cook for 25 to 30 minutes at 375 degrees F. Salt more if you like and serve.

—*Momma Ballzak, Lot #16*

MOMMA'S POTATO SALAD

This stuff is guaranteed to help heal any scrapes, cuts, or bruises that any little girl might get on May Day. Sorry, shocks of high voltage are not included in the list.

Makes 8 servin's

12 large potatoes, cut into medium-size cubes
2 tablespoons salt
12 eggs, hard-boiled and chopped
3 stalks celery
2 large dill pickles
2 cups Miracle Whip
¼ cup yellow table mustard

In a large pot, cover the potatoes with water and add the salt. Boil until the potatoes are tender when pierced with a fork. Put the potatoes, eggs, celery, and pickles in a large bowl. Mix together the Miracle Whip and mustard and stir until smooth. Pour this over the potato mixture and mix. Chill several hours or overnight before serving.

—Momma Boxcar, Lot #5

CONNIE KAY'S GOD BLESS AMERICA POTATO SALAD

Regardless of what the name might be, this salad is also tasty in Canada, Mexico, and any other part of the world.

Makes 6 servin's

5 potatoes, cut into small cubes
Red and blue food colorin'
2 eggs, hard-boiled and chopped
¼ cup diced celery
½ onion, diced
1 tablespoon diced pimientos
3 sweet pickles, diced into small pieces
1½ cups mayonnaise

Cook the potato cubes, drain, and divide in half. Mix a few drops of red food colorin' with one half, and mix a few drops of blue food colorin' into the other half. Cover each and put 'em in the freezer for 30 minutes.

In a big bowl, add the remainin' ingredients and mix with mayonnaise until nice and creamy. Add the potatoes and lightly toss. Cover and put in the fridge for 1 hour, or until the potatoes have thawed out.

—Connie Kay, Lot #13

GOD'S GOOD GREEN PEA SALAD

I'll give this dish an amen any day.

Makes 4 to 6 servin's

14 ounces green peas
2 eggs, hard-boiled and chopped
1 cup Velveeta cheese, cubed into tiny pieces
½ cup Spam, diced
2 tablespoon sweet pickle relish
1½ cups Miracle Whip

Mix it all together real good and chill for a few hours.

—*Pastor Ida May Bee, Lot #7*

GERMAN SPINACH

Wendy says her husband, Harry Bottom, came back from fightin' over in Europe durin' WWII with this recipe and a plate in his head. A bomb had gone off, actually drivin' a blue china plate right into the side of his skull. The doctors decided it would be too dangerous to try to remove it, so they left it in. At the church socials, Harry would always used that plate to carry items that wouldn't fit on the paper one he had in his hands.

Makes 6 servin's

2 tablespoons margarine
1 tablespoon onion flakes
1 clove garlic, crushed
20 ounces spinach, chopped, cooked, and drained
6 bacon strips, cooked and crumbled
¼ teaspoon nutmeg
½ teaspoon salt
⅛ teaspoon black pepper

Put your margarine, onion flakes, and garlic in a skillet and sauté for 1 minute. Add the rest of the ingredients and stir. Cover and cook on low heat for 10 to 15 minutes.

—*Wendy Bottom, Lot #4*

OLD-TIMER'S TATER SALAD

Regardless if you call it potato or tater, it's still darn good.

Makes 6 servin's

6 taters, cooked and cubed
3 eggs, hard-boiled and diced
1 medium onion, diced
3 stalks celery, diced

Toss together the taters, eggs, onion, and celery.

In a saucepan, combine the followin' ingredients:

1 cup sugar
1 tablespoon cornstarch
½ teaspoon salt
⅛ teaspoon pepper

Gradually add:

½ cup vinegar
½ cup water

Once you've made a smooth paste in the saucepan, add:

2 eggs, beaten

Cook till thickened. Remove from the heat and add:

1 teaspoon mustard
½ cup salad dressin' or Miracle Whip

Pour the hot mixture over the potato combo. Toss well and chill overnight. This is real yummy.

—*Lovie Birch, Lot #20*

MACARONI SALAD

Donna Sue says that when it comes to knowledge about small curved noodles, Vance is your man.

Makes 6 servin's

½ pound macaroni, uncooked
1¼ cups mayonnaise (regardless of what Vance says, Miracle Whip is
   fine instead)
1 teaspoon mustard
2 eggs, hard-boiled and chopped
1 (8 ¼-ounce) can crushed pineapple, well drained
1 (6-ounce) can chunk light tuna, well drained
1 teaspoon salt
½ teaspoon pepper

Cook the macaroni accordin' to the package directions; rinse under cold water and drain well.

In a medium bowl, combine the cooled macaroni, mayonnaise, mustard, eggs, pineapple, tuna, salt, and pepper; mix well. Adjust the mayonnaise and salt and pepper to taste. Chill in refrigerator thoroughly before servin'.

—*Vance Pool, Lot #19*

ANITA'S BAR AND GRILL CORN BREAD SALAD

This would get a Baptist into a bar, but thanks to Anita's new drive-up window, they don't have to worry.

Makes 4 to 6 servin's

2 (8-ounce) boxes corn bread mix
2 cups Miracle Whip
1 regular can kernel corn
1 green bell pepper, chopped
4 eggs, hard-boiled and chopped
6 green onions (includin' the tops), chopped

1 tomato, diced
2 cups grated cheddar cheese

Make the corn bread by followin' the package directions. Set aside to cool.
  Combine the Miracle Whip with the corn. Crumble up the corn bread into the corn mixture, then add the rest of the ingredients. Stir well. Cover and place in the fridge overnight to chill.

—Anita Biggon, Lot #2

MY CORNS CASSEROLE

This ain't got nothin' to do with your feet.

Makes 6 servin's

½ cup margarine, softened
1 cup dairy sour cream
1 egg
1 can whole-kernel corn, drained
1 can cream-style corn, undrained
1 package corn muffin mix
1 cup grated Cheddar cheese

Mix your margarine, sour cream, and egg together, then add your cans of corn and corn muffin mix. Stir it up real good and put it in a greased casserole dish. Bake for 45 minutes at 375 degrees F., put the cheese on it, and bake for 15 more minutes.

—Momma Boxcar, Lot #5

BETTER THAN PERFECT MASHED POTATOES

Accordin' to Donny and Kenny, these are to "die for."

Makes 6 to 8 servin's

6 potatoes, diced, boiled, and drained
½ cup buttermilk

½ teaspoon bakin' soda
Salt and pepper
2 tablespoons margarine

Mash the potatoes. Mix the buttermilk and bakin' soda together. Beat it into the potatoes. Season to taste with salt and pepper. Beat the margarine into the potatoes.

—Donny Owems, Lot #15

BORN-AGAIN BAKED BEANS

I actually saw Pastor Ida May Bee wolf down a whole bowl of these at a Sunday after-noon BBQ. Needless to say, church was canceled that night.

Makes 6 to 8 servin's

3 (16-ounce) cans pork 'n' beans
12 slices bacon
½ onion, coarsely chopped
¾ cup ketchup
2 tablespoons wienie (yellow) mustard
1 teaspoon minced garlic (the jar kind is much easier to use)
¾ cup brown sugar

Pour the cans of pork 'n' beans into a large glass casserole.

Slice the bacon slices into 1-inch pieces. You can either fry 'em till they're startin' to get crisp or use 'em raw (they'll cook in the beans). Add the bacon and onion to the beans and mix 'em up real good.

In a medium bowl, combine the ketchup, wienie mustard, minced garlic, and brown sugar. Mix well. Stir this mixture into the beans. Bake at 350 degrees F. for an hour or more dependin' on how thick you like your beans.

—Pastor Ida May Bee, Lot #7

Chapter 14

My sister, Donna Sue, and Ollie White and me get real corny with some tasty
BBQed corn on the cob.

Veggies

This year the fine folks at the High Chaparral all joined together and threw a big BBQ for the seniors at the Last Stop Nursing Home. We trailer folks have always regarded our elderly with love and joy regardless of the pain in the butts they might be from time to time. Sure they're usually in the way and are always needin' us to do somethin' for 'em at the most inopportune times, but we still love 'em. I know my sister and I would do anything for our Me-Ma, just as long as we don't have to touch her when she's naked and needs a bath. After all, she is our flesh and blood even though it may be badly wrinkled and ice-cold.

They got the seniors at the Last Stop Nursing Home, where Me-Ma resides, to fixin' up the place for the BBQ. They decorated the halls with balloons and streamers. And all the old folks got party hats to wear. In the dinin' area they served all of 'em punch and cake. It was really beautiful.

We lit up the BBQ around eleven in the mornin' and Ben Beaver and some of the menfolk took turns cookin'. We made some of the softer foods like the Last Stop Nursing Home Filet Mignon and grilled vegetables for 'em. Needless to say, they had a great time.

At one in the afternoon, the girls from the Blue Whale Strip Club came by before havin' to head off to work and did a few numbers. Some of the residents had to return to their rooms when the show ended on account of sheer exhaustion.

Since it's a proven fact that animals can help you live longer, as well as the idea that older folks relate to dogs and cats, the management arranged for four or five dogs to come to the nursin' home for the seniors to interact with. Course, all the residents were excited to play with the dogs. Most of them had grown up with dogs on the farm or in their houses. Yes, it was to be a fun-filled event for all involved. That was until the canines turned out to be retired police dogs. Oh, it was terrible! I've never seen anything like that in real life. To this day when I think about what happened, well, it just turns my stomach. Luckily they finally restrained the dogs before they could get to all the family members who'd been standin' in the smokin' lounge. I tell you what, though, the nursin' home was lucky that they didn't get sued. Who knows what those dogs could have caught with all the drugs some of those folks have to take. Next year they've decided to just bring in a mime.

BEFORE YOU GRILL VEGETABLES

There are a few things that you need to know about vegetables before you start grillin' 'em. Most veggies will dry out real fast from the fire, which is why it's always good to give 'em a good coatin' of oil before you place 'em on the BBQ. Personally, I like to then sprinkle 'em with some of the rub that I have handy. It adds an even better taste to these gifts from God.

Another thing to remember is that the denser vegetables tend to take longer to cook, just like thicker pieces of meat. This means that you will want to most likely keep bastin' those vegetables a bit more as they cook.

Lots of people used to wrap their vegetables in foil before cookin', which is fine, but now that the grill woks and even grill toppers are easier to find, you can use those to get a more BBQ'd taste. But either way is fine.

DONNA SUE'S GRILLED CORN ON THE COB

I know it sounds crazy, but this really is pretty dang tasty.

Makes 4 servin's

4 ears of corn
1 can beer

3 tablespoons margarine, melted

1 teaspoon pancake syrup, warm

Carefully pull the husks back so that you can get out all the silk. Set the corn aside.

Mix the remainin' ingredients together and pour into a loaf pan. Take your corn and dip 'em in the mixture. Wrap the corn back up with the husks, and place 'em on the grill. Cook for about 15 minutes, turnin' occasionally. Serve hot.

—Donna Sue Boxcar, Lot #6

CONNIE KAY'S SWEET CORN

The secret is in the water!

Makes 1–20 ears of corn

1 to 20 ears of corn

3 cups sugar

Enough water to cover the corn

Take each ear and peel back the husk. Remove the silk and place the ear down in a bucket like those white ones that you can find in a hardware store. Just make sure your bucket is big enough so the actual corn cob part goes all the way in. Set aside.

Take a bowl and pour in the sugar. Add 4 cups hot water to cover the sugar. Mix until most of the sugar dissolves. Pour into the bucket. Fill the bucket up with water from your garden hose. Put the corn in the bucket, cover the bucket, and let set for 1 to 1½ hours. Pull the corn out of the bucket and cover each ear back up with its very own husk. Place on the grill and cook for 5 minutes on each side.

—Connie Kay, Lot #13

ANITA BIGGON'S WILD GRILLED POTATOES

If you think this is wild, you should see Anita after a few Southern Comfort shots.

Makes 4 potatoes

4 potatoes, cleaned with the skin still on
4 teaspoons margarine
4 teaspoons vegetable oil
2 teaspoons seasonin' salt
4 tablespoons Worcestershire sauce

Take your potatoes and slit 'em down the middle, bein' careful not to cut 'em in half. For each potato, put a teaspoon of margarine right dab in the middle of it. Take a teaspoon of oil and pour it on the outside of the potato. Rub the oil all over the potato and place it over a foot-long piece of foil. Sprinkle 1 teaspoon of seasonin' salt on the potato, allowin' the extra salt to fall on the foil. Place the potato on the foil and fold it halfway. Pour on 1 tablespoon of the Worcestershire sauce and finish wrappin' it up. Place the wrapped potatoes on a hot grill to BBQ for 30 to 45 minutes, or until they are soft.

—Anita Biggon, Lot #2

Chapter 15

LeRoy and Harry set back with Momma Ballzak and enjoy the summer sun, while Vance applies a layer of Momma Ballzak's Slap Me Silly Sauce to his meat.

Sauces, Glazes, Marinades, and Rubs

When you go from trailer lot to trailer lot here at the High Chaparral, en-joyin' the BBQ foods that your neighbor has prepared, you quickly learn that there are five very important things that make each lot special.

1. The Sauces
2. The Glazes
3. The Marinades
4. The Rubs
5. Usin' meat that ain't expired (I swear Lulu Bell is gonna kill some-body if she don't pay more attention to them stickers on the meat before she buys it).

All these are items are very important, especially number five, but what I want to do in this chapter is to focus on numbers one to four. Since each region of the country has kind of taken the fine art of BBQin' and put its own spin on it, there are lots of different types of sauces. And as many of us residents from the High Chaparral have had the opportunity to travel around, we've kind of brought back some of those different tastes with us, especially when it comes to our BBQ sauces. So have fun with these recipes and enjoy tryin' some new tastes that you might not have tried before. I'm sure one of these will eventually turn out to be a staple for your family when you BBQ.

Now I've divided this chapter up into sauces, glazes, marinades, and rubs, and I tell you at the start of each section a little about what they are and how they work. So before you start usin' 'em, please make sure to read the openin' from each portion.

SAUCES

Sauces are kind of like the men you'll find in a trailer park. They all have one thing in common, but they're still all different. Some are hot and spicy, while others are robust and full of flavor. They come in all different colors, and from all different backgrounds. And if you ain't careful, there are those that'll slap you into next week before you know what hit you (see the Hell Fire and Damnation Sauce).

Sauces have two main purposes. One of those is to set the slightly burnt coatin' on the outside of your food while moisturizin' the meat at the same time. And of course, the sauces with tomatoes and sugars have to be watched, 'cause they can burn very easily if exposed to the heat for too long, which is why they should only be applied to cookin' foods five to fifteen minutes before the meat is done. The other purpose of sauces is to complement the meat after it's been cooked.

So regardless of what you like in your sauces, give these a try. Remember that it's better to experiment at home. It costs a lot less, and if you don't like it, you can pour it into a container and give it to your neighbor as a present.

And don't forget that you can take all your extra sauce, pour it into ice trays, cover it, and let it freeze. Then just put these cubes in a big plastic bag and keep 'em in the freezer. This way your sauce don't go bad, and when you're ready to use it, you can just pull out the amount you'll need and stick it in the microwave. So have fun and enjoy.

GRAPE KETCHUP

I've had many folks ask me to check with the gang at the High Chaparral for this recipe. Well, wouldn't you know Wendy Bottom would know this one.

Makes several pints

2 quarts ripe seedless grapes
Enough mild vinegar to cover the grapes
1 cup granulated sugar
1 tablespoon cinnamon

1 tablespoon allspice
1 tablespoon ground cloves
¼ tablespoon cayenne pepper

Put your grapes in a large pot and pour in the vinegar. Cook on a medium heat until the grapes are soft. Rub through a sieve, then add the sugar and spices. Cook on low until it gets thick like regular ketchup. Pour the mixture into sterilized pint-size jars and seal. This is great on anythin'.

—*Wendy Bottom, Lot #4*

CHARLIE CHASE YOU 'ROUND THE ROOM TONIGHT SAUCE

I like that Charlie Chase. He really is nice, kind, and funny. This is in his honor, or at least what's left of it after havin' me on that mornin' show he does in Nashville.

Makes 4½ to 5 cups

2 cups water
1 cup ketchup
½ cup brown sugar
½ cup vinegar
½ tablespoon Worcestershire sauce
1 onion, finely chopped
½ teaspoon salt

Mix it all together in a pot and let it simmer till it gets good and thick.

—*Ruby Ann Boxcar, Lot #18*

RIDE 'EM COWBOY SAUCE

The local Vo-Ag group uses this sauce on all the BBQ they cook at their annual Rodeo Night Fund-raiser.

Makes about 3 cups

1 cup ketchup
½ cup water

⅓ cup vinegar
¾ cup sugar
3 tablespoons cornstarch
2 tablespoons soy sauce
2 teaspoons onion powder
1½ teaspoons paprika
1 teaspoon garlic powder
½ teaspoon pepper

In a large pan, combine all the ingredients and simmer for 30 minutes, stirrin' often.

—*Buck N. Hiney, Lot #1*

DR PEPPER BBQ SAUCE

My husband, Dew, drinks this one straight out of the bottle.

Makes about 2 ½ cups

1 onion, chopped
1 cup ketchup
½ cup Dr Pepper
½ cup water
¼ cup vinegar
¼ cup margarine
2½ tablespoons Worcestershire sauce
2 tablespoons sugar
1 tablespoon lemon juice
1½ teaspoons salt
½ teaspoon black pepper
¼ teaspoon cayenne pepper

Mix all of this together on the stove and let it simmer for 15 to 20 minutes. Stir occasionally.

—*Mickey Ray Kay, Lot #13*

JUANITA'S LEMON BUTTER SAUCE

Leave it to dear Juanita to come up with such a tasty sauce on such a limited budget.

Makes about 1 cup

6 tablespoons margarine
6 teaspoons lemon juice
¼ teaspoon garlic powder
⅛ teaspoon salt

Put the margarine in a saucepan and heat until it melts. Add the rest of the ingredients and cook on a medium heat until it boils, reduce heat and simmer for 5 minutes, stirrin' from time to time. Set aside and serve warm on any kind of meat. This also makes a great bastin' sauce.

—*Juanita Hix, Lot #9*

WHERE THE HECK AM I JOAN BBQ SAUCE

Momma Ballzak named this after the gal who does all the schedulin' for my book signin's. She always takes real good care of me and my personal assistant when we're on the road.

Makes 2½ cups

1 cup red wine
2 small cans tomato paste
2 teaspoons salt
2 teaspoons sugar
1½ teaspoons chili powder
1 teaspoon dry mustard
1 teaspoon paprika
1 teaspoon pepper
1 teaspoon bay leaf
1 teaspoon cumin

In a saucepan, mix all ingredients and cook over medium heat for 20 minutes, stirring now and then so it doesn't burn. Reduce heat to low and simmer for 10 more minutes.

—*Momma Ballzak, Lot #16*

TRAILER PARK SAUCE

Yes, folks, this is the official BBQ sauce of trailer parks across the world.

Makes 4 cups

1 cup ketchup
1 cup minced onions, sautéed
½ cup water
¼ cup lemon juice
¼ cup Worcestershire sauce
¼ cup brown sugar
2 tablespoons yellow mustard
2 teaspoons salt
½ teaspoon pepper

Mix it all up in a pot and simmer for 1 hour, or just 15 minutes if you're in a real big hurry.

—*Momma Boxcar, Lot #5*

LULU BELL'S SIMPLE SAUCE

Simple, yes, but her boyfriend sure loves this stuff.

Makes about 6 cups

1 regular bottle ketchup
1 regular bottle A.1. sauce
1 regular bottle Heinz 57 sauce
1 cup brown sugar

Mix well and simmer for 10 minutes till warm.

—*Lulu Bell Boxcar, Lot #8*

MOMMA BALLZAK'S SLAP ME SILLY SAUCE

This one'll get you locked up!

Makes about 4 cups

1 regular can tomato soup
½ cup finely diced onions
½ cup sweet pickle juice
¼ cup brown sugar
2 tablespoons Worcestershire sauce
1 cup bourbon

Mix the first five ingredients together in a pan. Bring to a boil. Take off the heat and let set for 10 minutes. Add the bourbon. Stir well and drink . . . I mean use on your food.

—*Momma Ballzak, Lot #16*

HOLY MOLY BBQ SAUCE

You might as well chew on an electric fence!

Makes 2½ to 3 cups

½ cup ketchup
½ cup lemon juice
⅓ cup white vinegar
¼ cup water
2 tablespoons brown sugar
2 tablespoons vegetable oil
1 tablespoon hot sauce
1 teaspoon paprika
1 teaspoon cayenne pepper
1 teaspoon soy sauce
½ teaspoon onion powder

½ teaspoon garlic powder
½ teaspoon black pepper

Mix everything together in a big pan and simmer for 1 hour.

—*Hubert Bunch, Lot #3*

CONNIE KAY'S RHUBARB STEAK SAUCE

No, this ain't one of Me-Ma's recipes. I don't know where Connie picked this recipe up at, but it sure is good.

Makes 14 cups

8 cups chopped rhubarb
4 cups diced onion
2 cups vinegar
2⅓ cups dark brown sugar, packed
1 teaspoon ground cinnamon
1 teaspoon allspice
½ teaspoon ground cloves
1 teaspoon salt
½ teaspoon pepper

Mix everythin' up in a big pot and put it on the fire. Bring the mixture to a boil, then turn your heat down and let simmer for about an hour. Allow it to cool, pour it into bottles or containers, and store some in the fridge for easy access and the rest in the freezer. I like to be able to grab a new bottle from the freezer when I see we're gettin' low in the fridge. This is great on beef.

—*Connie Kay, Lot #13*

OPAL LAMB-INMAN'S BBQ SAUCE

They ought to bottle this stuff up and sell it at the Super Store.

Makes around 2 quarts

¼ cup dark brown sugar
2 tablespoons chili powder
1 clove garlic, crushed
5 dashes of ginger
5 dashes of oregano
5 dashes of paprika
5 dashes of turmeric
5 dashes of marjoram
1 teaspoon ground mustard
1 (12-ounce) bottle ketchup
4 (8-ounce) cans tomato sauce
1 cup dill pickle vinegar
½ cup sweet pickle vinegar
5 tablespoons Worcestershire sauce
3 cups water

Mix the first nine ingredients together in a large bowl. Next, simply add the rest of the ingredients and mix well. As long as you keep it in the fridge, this stuff will keep indefinitely.

—*Opal Lamb-Inman, Lot #1*

MARGARET'S CORRECTIONS SAUCE

This is named after my editor, and it works like she does. Regardless of how dry or tough your meat might be, this sauce makes it come alive.

Makes about 6 ½ cups

2 cups ketchup
1 cup margarine

1 cup vegetable oil
¾ cup lemon juice
¾ cup brown sugar
½ cup diced onion
¼ cup Worcestershire sauce
6 tablespoons minced garlic
2 tablespoons Tabasco sauce
1 tablespoon black pepper
2 teaspoons chili powder
2 teaspoons salt
2 teaspoons red pepper flakes
1 teaspoon dry mustard

Put in a pot, mix well, and simmer for 5 minutes.

—Ruby Ann Boxcar, Lot #18

EASTERNER BBQ SAUCE

I didn't know Tina'd been out East, but this sauce is so good, I really don't care!

Makes 3 to 4 cups

2 cups white vinegar
2 sticks margarine
2 tablespoons salt
2 tablespoons crushed red pepper flakes
5 teaspoons black pepper
2 tablespoons lemon juice
2 tablespoons sugar

Mix all together and simmer on low heat a while. That's it! It keeps in the fridge almost forever.

—Tina Faye Stopenblotter, Lot #17

RC COLA SAUCE

Believe it or not, this here is real tasty on just about any old meat.

Makes 3 to 4 cups

1 can RC cola
1 regular bottle ketchup
1 teaspoon garlic salt
⅛ teaspoon liquid smoke

Mix it all together and let simmer for 20 minutes on a low heat.

—*Elroy Dasafe, Lot #19*

BRUCE'S CITRUS DILL SAUCE

Bruce is the nicest, sweetest, most carin' man in New York City. Did I mention as well that he makes sure I get my royalty checks?

Makes about 2 ½ cups

½ cup light brown sugar
½ cup light Karo syrup
¼ cup dill pickle juice
1 can orange soda pop
1 teaspoon yellow mustard
1 teaspoon soy sauce

In a large bowl, mix the brown sugar, Karo syrup, and dill pickle juice together. Add the orange soda pop, mustard, and soy sauce. Mix well. Put on the stove and simmer for 10 minutes.

—*Ollie White, Lot #10*

HELLFIRE AND DAMNATION SAUCE

This sauce of Sister Bertha's is so hot it'd make the devil cry!

Makes 5 to 6 cups

4 dried habanero peppers
4 jalapeño peppers
1¾ cups water
2 cups ketchup
1 cup tomato paste
⅓ cup apple cider vinegar
1½ teaspoons cayenne pepper
1 teaspoon hot sauce
½ teaspoon cumin
½ teaspoon turmeric
½ cup brown sugar
2 tablespoons soy sauce

Dice up the peppers and keep the seeds. Place the seeds and peppers in a saucepan and add the water. Bring to a boil, then reduce heat. Add the rest of the ingredients, stir, and simmer for 30 minutes. Put it in the fridge overnight. Taste the next day. You might need a bit more salt or a teaspoon of sugar dependin' on your personal taste.

—*Sister Bertha, Lot #12*

WALTER AND STEVE'S SWEET BBQ SAUCE

Them boys are as good and sweet as this BBQ sauce, which makes it hard for me to tell 'em that I think my sister, Donna Sue, wants 'em real bad.

Makes 6½ to 7 cups

1 shot whiskey
4½ cups ketchup
¾ cup white vinegar

3 tablespoons chili powder
½ cup molasses
¼ cup water
1½ cups brown sugar
2 teaspoons liquid smoke
2 teaspoons dry mustard
½ teaspoon ginger
½ teaspoon allspice
½ teaspoon flour
¼ teaspoon cayenne pepper
¼ teaspoon black pepper

Mix it all together in a pan and simmer for 30 to 45 minutes, watchin' that it don't stick on the bottom.

—Donna Sue Boxcar, Lot #6

LULU BELL'S LEMON-LIME BBQ SAUCE

This will give your meat a refreshin' taste.

Makes 6 to 7 cups

3 cups ketchup
1 can Sprite
¾ cup pancake syrup
½ cup margarine
1 cup diced onions
2 tablespoons Worcestershire sauce
1 tablespoon minced garlic
1 teaspoon salt

Mix well and simmer for 1 hour.

—Lulu Bell Boxcar, Lot #8

BOURBON STREET BBQ SAUCE

I got a feelin' Faye Faye knew every inch of Bourbon Street back when she used to live there, if you know what I mean.

Makes 1¾ to 2 cups

1 cup ketchup
½ cup bourbon
⅓ cup maple syrup
¼ cup vegetable oil
2 tablespoons cider vinegar
2 tablespoon honey Dijon–style mustard

No need to heat this one up, just mix it all together. Great for both chicken and ribs.

—*Faye Faye Larue, Lot #17*

URI'S TKEMALI SAUCE

Accordin' to Uri, this here stuff is to Russia what ketchup is to America.

Makes about 2 cups

½ pound plums
1 peeled garlic clove
2 tablespoons chopped cilantro
2 teaspoons dill
2 teaspoons basil
1 teaspoon salt
1 tablespoon lemon juice

Place the plums in a small pan and add just enough water to cover 'em. Cook till the water boils. Reduce the heat and let 'em cook for another 10 minutes, stirrin' occasionally. Cook for 10 more minutes, stirrin' constantly. Pour through a strainer, keepin' the juice. Set everything aside for a few minutes. When you come back, pit the prunes. Throw the pits away and put the prunes in a blender. Blend until they are puréed. Add that juice that you saved to the blender a little at a time. Keep the blender goin' as you add the juice. You want it to be as thick as cream. Throw the rest of the juice away. Stop the blender and pour the purée out into a pan. Add the rest of the ingredients and stir well. Put on the stove and bring it to a boil. Stir constantly. Take it off the heat, set it aside, and let it cool. Then pour it into mason jar or empty bottle.

—Uri Krochichin, Lot #1

KEN'S FAMOUS BBQ SAUCE

This is actually one of the fellas that Donna Sue met while she and the other girls from the Blue Whale Strip Club were out performin' their civic duty of makin' sure every prisoner gets a conjugal visit regardless if they want one or not.

Makes 6 to 6½ cups

1 (28-ounce) bottle ketchup
1 cup dill pickle juice
⅓ cup dark brown sugar
¼ cup Worcestershire sauce
2 tablespoons vegetable oil
1 tablespoon yellow mustard
1 tablespoon vinegar
3 teaspoons chili powder
2 heapin' teaspoons garlic powder
2 teaspoons liquid smoke
1 heapin' teaspoon chopped chives
½ teaspoon cumin

Mix 'em up, simmer for 15 to 20 minutes, and bottle.

—Donna Sue Boxcar, Lot #6

LAURIE'S ONE HOT SEXY MOMMA BBQ SAUCE

Laurie is another one of them publishin' gals that I just love to death, and the title says it all. I think Lois has caught her in a bottle.

Makes about 3 cups

⅓ cup molasses
⅓ cup brewed coffee
¾ cup ketchup
¼ cup cider vinegar
¼ cup Worcestershire sauce
3 tablespoons chili powder
3 tablespoons Tabasco sauce
1 tablespoon vegetable oil
2 teaspoons dry mustard
1 teaspoon soy sauce

Mix well and simmer for 1 hour. Pour into a bottle.

—*Lois Bunch, Lot #3*

GLAZES

Now glazes work a lot like sauces except that their main purpose is to be applied to the BBQin' item while it's on the grill. Since they all got sugar in' 'em, they tend to burn faster. Since most of us don't smoke our foods, but rather cook 'em quickly, we have to be careful with glazes or we'll end up with a burnt piece of meat that ain't done enough for us on the inside. So what we do is use glaze on the last ten to five minutes on an item. Play with your glazes, 'cause they sure do add a nice taste and look to your food, but at the same time, watch real close to make sure that your glaze ain't burnin'.

PRANCIN' PIG GLAZE

No, this was not named for my sister by a Peepin' Tom. None of those men have lived to tell their tale. LOL!

Makes 1 to 1½ cups

¾ cup molasses
½ cup honey mustard
2 tablespoons pepper
2 tablespoons mustard
¼ teaspoon allspice
3 tablespoons sherry

Combine the first five ingredients together in a pan and heat till it boils. Reduce the heat and let it set for 6 minutes. Stir. Add the sherry. Stir. Take off of heat.

—Momma Ballzak, Lot #16

TINA FAYE'S BURGER GLAZE

I'd have never thought about glazin' a simple little old hamburger, but this is real good stuff.

Makes ¾ cup

½ cup ketchup
¼ cup mustard (whichever one happens to be on sale is just fine)
½ teaspoon hot sauce

Mix 'em all up real good and brush on your burgers as they BBQ.

—Tina Faye Stopenblotter, Lot #17

DOUG'S GO-GO-GO GLAZE

Doug makes sure that stores know that they need my books. I sure am glad he's on my side, I can tell you that.

Makes 2½ to 3 cups

1 teaspoon apple vinegar
3 tablespoons dark brown sugar
1⅜ cups ketchup
1 cup water
3 tablespoons Worcestershire sauce
1 teaspoon salt
Dash of pepper

Pour your vinegar into a bowl and microwave it for 1 minute on high. Add the brown sugar and stir well until the sugar dissolves. Add the ketchup, water, Worcestershire, salt, and pepper. Mix well. Put it in a pan and bring it to a boil. Cook for 8 minutes, stirrin' constantly.

—*Kenny Lynn, Lot #15*

KITTY'S GLAZE

Sometimes she'll bring a bottle of this stuff to the church BBQ, but you know she don't tell nobody that it has beer in it. The funny part is that Sister Bertha keeps buggin' her for the recipe.

Makes about 3½ cups

1 cup honey
2 tablespoons margarine
2 teaspoons chili powder
1 teaspoon crushed red pepper
1 long-neck bottle beer

Mix the first four ingredients together in a pan and heat for 5 minutes on low, stirrin' constantly. Add the beer and simmer for 30 minutes.

—*Kitty Chitwood, Lot #11*

MOMMA BOXCAR'S EASY GLAZE

Momma wanted to call this her Easy Glaze, but I told her that people might think it was one of Me-Ma's recipes.

Makes 1 cup

½ cup honey
½ cup Opal Lamb-Inman's BBQ Sauce (page 140)

Stir together and simmer for 10 minutes.

—Momma Boxcar, Lot #5

ME-MA'S BBQ SAUCE

Oh the pain! Please don't try this at home.

Makes too much

1 regular jar jalapeño peppers
1 regular bottle BBQ sauce from store
2 cups powdered sugar
6 teaspoons cayenne pepper

Mix real good and serve.

—Me-Ma, Formerly of Lot #8

MARINADES

When it comes to marinades, you're gonna start off by piercin' your meat so the marinade can get into it. Thinner cuts of meat do better with marinades than the thicker cuts do. Personally all of us at the High Chaparral like to let our meat set in the fridge soakin' up all that juice for at least eight hours. If you can wait a whole day or two, then that's even better. Just remember that if you turn around and use your marinade as a sauce with the meal, boil it for five minutes to make sure and kill all that nasty bacteria that came from soakin' raw meat in it. Don't use the marinade as a glaze or mop on your meat while it's cookin', or you'll have to keep cookin' the meat in order to kill that bacteria. If you boil the marinade first, that's fine just as long as you don't dip your brush back into the marinade or you will contaminate your boiled marinade with the juices from the meat.

To make a marinade, just combine all the ingredients in each recipe. The order don't matter, just as long as you got 'em all mixed up real good. Next, put your meat in a plastic bag and then pour the mixture over top of it. Get all the air out of your bag and seal it nice and tight. Put it in the fridge. Turn the bag every half hour so the marinade gets to all of the meat. Now if you're gonna lay down and go to bed at night, turn it every ten minutes durin' the hour before your bedtime. In the mornin' before you do anythin', turn that darn bag over and start the thirty-minute process again till it's time to cook. If for some reason you can't be home with your meat, then turn it as often as you can when you are at home.

DOTTIE'S MARINADE

She sells this at her store for $2 a bottle. If you feel guilty about makin' it at home and not buyin' it, then by all means, make it and send me the $2.

Makes a little over 2 cups

2 cups olive oil
Juice and pulp of 1 lemon
1 tablespoon kosher salt

—*Dottie Lamb, Lot #14*

MARY'S MARINADE

This one is in honor of my favorite Italian in the book industry!

Makes a little more than 1 cup

½ cup lemon juice
½ cup olive oil
2 cloves garlic, crushed

¼ teaspoon salt
¼ teaspoon pepper
¼ teaspoon oregano

—*Ruby Ann Boxcar, Lot #18*

MOMMA BALLZAK'S JUST RIGHT MARINADE

I got to admit, steaks soaked in this marinade taste great, but stand back and make sure you use the long tongs when you put the meat on the grill.

Makes a lot, but after a few minutes in the marinade, the meat don't really care.

1 bottle tequila
1 tablespoon garlic powder
2 teaspoons salt
1 teaspoon thyme
¼ teaspoon pepper
Dash of paprika

—*Momma Ballzak, Lot #16*

I THINK I'M TURNIN' JAPANESE MARINADE

This helps enhance our taste for Asian food.

Makes 2 ½ cups

10 ounces teriyaki sauce
1 teaspoon garlic salt
1 can beer

—*Anita Biggon, Lot #2*

OPAL'S LAMB JUICE

Opal says Dick just loves this brushed on his lamb.

Makes about ½ cup

2 tablespoons soy sauce
4 teaspoons sesame oil
2 green onions, diced
2 cloves garlic, minced
2 teaspoons minced gingerroot
¼ teaspoon black pepper

—Opal Lamb-Inman, Lot #1

ANITA BRYANT MARINADE

This will chew the tough right out of your rump roast.

Makes 3 cups

1 (12-ounce) can thawed orange juice concentrate
½ cup molasses
½ cup soy sauce
2 teaspoons powdered ginger
1 teaspoon honey

—Donny Owens, Lot #15

JAVA JUICE MARINADE

A little rain and a steak cooked in this and you'd swear you was in Seattle.

Makes 3 to 4 cups

2 garlic cloves, chopped
3 cups strong coffee

2 tablespoons lemon juice
2 tablespoons olive oil
2 tablespoons red wine
1½ teaspoons dried rosemary
1 teaspoon salt
½ teaspoon pepper

—*Wendy Bottom, Lot #4*

THE CHEEKY CHICKEN MARINADE

This marinade will make your chicken sing.

used on a whole
chicken-inside.
with 3T. butter, lemon,
onion, garlic, inside.
Baked.

Makes little less than 1 cup

6 tablespoons soy sauce
6 tablespoons Worcestershire sauce
2 tablespoons oil
1 teaspoon garlic powder
1 teaspoon pepper

—*Wanda Kay, Lot #13*

DR PEPPER MARINADE

I've said it before and I'll say it again, my husband, Dew, sure does love his Dr Pepper.

Makes 4 to 4½ cups

1 can Dr Pepper
2 cups ketchup
6 tablespoons Worcestershire sauce
2 tablespoons dried oregano
1 minced clove garlic

—*Dew Ballzak, Lot #18*

KITTY CHITWOOD'S DAMN 21-YEAR-OLD DR PEPPER MARINADE

Oh my goodness, Kitty Chitwood is at it again!

Makes 4 cups

1 can beer
1 can Dr Pepper
1 shot Hot Damn (a red cinnamon schnapps)
2 teaspoons hot sauce

—*Kitty Chitwood, Lot #11*

MOUNTAIN DEW MARINADE

I have to keep this out of Me-Ma's reach or she'll drink it before we get a chance to cook with it.

Makes 6 cups

4 cups Mountain Dew
2 cups vinegar

—*Harry Lombardi, Lot #19*

NELLIE TINKLE'S MELODY MARINADE

I know a big old steak after it's been marinated in some of this stuff and then BBQ'd will put a song in my heart.

Makes 2 to 2½ cups

1 regular bottle Italian salad dressin'
½ cup diced onions
½ cup Tang
2 tablespoons Worcestershire sauce

2 tablespoons hot sauce
1 tablespoon minced garlic
½ teaspoon salt
½ teaspoon pepper

—Nellie Tinkle, Lot #4

TRAILER PARK MARINADE

I can't begin to tell you how many times Momma used this one and then served it as sauce to boot.

Makes around 10 cups

1 regular bottle ketchup
1 regular bottle steak sauce
1 regular bottle Catalina dressin'
2 cups of your favorite BBQ sauce
1 can beer
¼ cup Worcestershire sauce
4 tablespoons honey
2 tablespoons minced onion

—Momma Boxcar, Lot #5

RUBS

Whichever rub you use, it works by sealin' in the flavor of the meat, and it does this by formin' a nice crust on the outside of the steak, burger, lamb chop, pork loin, chicken breast, or whatever type and piece of meat you're cookin'. Since your rub takes the moisture or dew from the air and pulls the juices from the inside of your meat, it basically creates it's own marinade. So unlike with marinade, you will not need or want to pierce your meat before applyin' your rub. And most rubs can last a good long time if kept in a dark dry place.

A lot of folks ask me what I like to use, rubs or marinades. Well, I have to honestly say that I love dry rubs, and I'll tell you why. They're just plain simple, like my niece, Lulu Bell. As long as you got the right amount of salt in there, you really can't go wrong. And once your dry rub starts workin' and you get a good osmosis goin' on with your meat, you can't beat it. You're sure to get a nice crust on the outside and a terrific taste on the inside.

Rubs are extremely easy to prepare. All you do is combine the listed ingredients in a bowl. When you get ready to use 'em, you can either pour the mixture into a seasonin' shaker and then sprinkle it over the meat, or you can simply take a bit of the mixture in your hand and sprinkle it on the meat that way. Just remember to be generous with your rub. Gently rub the sprinkle mixture into the meat. Then loosely wrap it up in foil or butcher paper and throw it in the fridge so it can work its magic for two or three day's time. Each of the followin' recipes make enough rub for twenty-four to thirty-two ounces of meat.

LULU BELL'S DROPPED ON YOUR HEAD RUB

Lulu Bell swears that after one bite of meat that you've used this rub on, you'll feel like somebody dropped you on your head. Trust me, she would know what that feels like, if you get my meanin', God bless her.

1¾ teaspoon seasoned salt
4 teaspoons lemon pepper
Dash of cayenne pepper
1 teaspoon garlic powder

—*Lulu Bell Boxcar, Lot #8*

KANSAS CITY GOOD TIME RUB

It's almost like bein' there!

2 cups sugar
¼ cup paprika
2 teaspoons chili seasonin'

½ teaspoon cayenne pepper
½ cup salt
2 teaspoons black pepper
1 teaspoon garlic powder

—*Pastor Ida May Bee, Lot #7*

RUB MY CHICKEN

This is also good on most any bird.

1½ tablespoons packed dark brown sugar
1½ teaspoons chili powder
¾ teaspoon garlic powder
¾ teaspoon paprika
½ teaspoon kosher salt
½ teaspoon onion powder
½ teaspoon cumin
¼ teaspoon cinnamon
¼ teaspoon black pepper
⅛ teaspoon cayenne pepper

—*Dick Inman, Lot #1*

GATOR RUB

Now, this ain't for use on gators, but rather on beef. Faye Faye says this rub is big in Louisiana.

½ teaspoon onion powder
½ teaspoon black pepper
½ teaspoon cayenne pepper
½ teaspoon crushed red pepper
½ teaspoon white pepper
¼ teaspoon salt

—*Faye Faye Larue, Lot #17*

ANY OLD MEAT WILL DO RUB

Thank you, Donna Sue.

1 teaspoon paprika
1 teaspoon coriander
1 teaspoon cumin
1 teaspoon dark brown sugar
1 teaspoon salt
1 teaspoon pepper

—Donna Sue Boxcar, Lot #6

SOUTH OF THE BORDER RUB

This will put the asa in your casa!

1 teaspoon black pepper
2 teaspoons cayenne pepper
2 teaspoons chili powder
2 teaspoons cumin
2 teaspoons brown sugar
1 teaspoon ground oregano
4 teaspoons paprika
2 teaspoons salt
1 teaspoon granulated sugar
1 teaspoon white pepper

—Lois Bunch, Lot #3

DIXIE SNOW RUB

This will give your meat a fantastically incredible taste that's as rare as Dixie snow. Speakin' of which, Faye Faye informs me that Dixie Snow will be joinin' the cast at the Danglin' Tassel later this year.

2 tablespoons salt
2 tablespoons granulated sugar
2 tablespoons dark brown sugar
2 tablespoons cumin
1 tablespoon ancho chile powder
1 tablespoon pasilla chile powder
1 tablespoon freshly cracked black pepper
1 tablespoon cayenne pepper
4 tablespoons paprika

—*Faye Faye Larue, Lot #17*

BEAVER RUB

Ben Beaver recommends this for fish, not beavers.

2 cloves garlic, minced
1 tablespoon olive oil
1 teaspoon rosemary
1 teaspoon thyme
1 teaspoon parsley flakes
½ teaspoon salt

—*Ben Beaver, Lot #14*

SISTER BERTHA'S REVIVAL RUB

Pastor Ida May Bee has Sister Bertha BBQ every night durin' a revival with a promise of a free meal after church to all who attend. Needless to say, Pastor Ida packs the pews Monday through Friday durin' one of these week-long rallies.

2 tablespoons salt
1 tablespoon garlic powder
1 tablespoon onion powder
1 tablespoon ground bay leaf
1 teaspoon thyme
1 teaspoon pepper

—Sister Bertha, Lot #12

RUB YOU THE RIGHT WAY RUB

You almost don't need no sauce after you've used this on your meat.

1 cup paprika
½ cup chili powder
½ cup cumin
1 teaspoon black pepper
½ teaspoon cayenne pepper
¼ cup sugar
2 tablespoons thyme
2 tablespoons garlic powder
2 tablespoons onion powder
1 tablespoon salt

—Lovie Birch, Lot #20

MARY HAD A LITTLE RUB

This is real good on lamb if you use it generously. This makes more than enough for twenty-four ounces of meat, so put it in a shaker and keep it in the cupboard.

1 tablespoon salt
1 tablespoon granulated sugar
1 tablespoon light brown sugar
1½ tablespoons cumin
2 tablespoons chili powder
2 tablespoons black pepper
½ tablespoon cayenne pepper
¼ cup paprika

—Donny Owens, Lot #15

LITTLE PIGGY RUB

Even though we get all the ingredients down at the Piggly Wiggly, this rub is in no way connected to the Piggly Wiggly.

2 tablespoons garlic powder
2 tablespoons dry mustard
2 tablespoons paprika
2 tablespoons salt
1 cup dark brown sugar

—Harland Hix, Lot #9

IN THE GARDEN RUB

If this here rub don't bless your meat, then nothin' will.

¼ teaspoon black pepper
½ teaspoon rosemary
½ teaspoon dry mustard

¾ teaspoon thyme
¾ teaspoon oregano

—Pastor Ida May Bee, Lot #7

TACO TACKLE SHACK'S EL RUBO

You'll be runnin' for more than the border with this stuff.

2 teaspoons chili powder
½ teaspoon cumin
½ teaspoon onion salt
¼ teaspoon garlic salt
⅛ teaspoon oregano

—Lois Bunch, Lot #3

Chapter 16

Lucky Kitty Chitwood gets to carry Dottie Lamb's traditional bowl of ambrosia salad over to the servin' table while her husband, Kyle, shows off his big tool durin' a recent High Chapparal Trailer Park BBQ.

Desserts

I'll never forget my very first boyfriend. His name was Rickey Boweevil, and he was a doll. He kind of looked like a young James Dean. Of course we was both young. I was in fourth grade and Rickey was in special ed. I took a lot of teasin' from my classmates for datin' him, but let me tell you, that boy could kiss. He had a tongue like a snake. Now I don't mean it was forked or nothin' like that, but just that he had full control of it, and could make it dodge and dart all over your mouth. So as you can imagine, with a talent like that, this little girl was able to easily ignore the teasin' and the fact that he always smelt like petroleum jelly. Anyways, when I'd walk him home every day after school, his momma would always have some kind of dessert waitin' for us. And trust me when I say that lady could cook. Everythin' she made was always out of this world. And I don't know if she did this 'cause I dated her son or if she was tryin' to cut down on her grocery bill and wanted my momma to feed me, but she gave me copies of every one of her dessert recipes. I don't know where Rickey's momma is today, since he broke up with me when I went into high school, but I still think of her every time I see the faces of my neighbors light up at our BBQs as they enjoy her desserts. Last I heard about my first love and what he was up to was three years ago, when somebody said that he was a political advisor and speechwriter for George W. Bush. That alone tells me that our relationship never would have worked out. And I'm not surprised he got a job that involved speech. Like I said, he was always good with his tongue.

By the way, before we dive into the desserts, let me give you a few helpful hints. If your dessert is supposed to be served cold, either wait to bring it outside, or make sure you got it wrapped up real good with foil and store it in a cooler with ice. Since some of these dishes have mayonnaise or milk in 'em, you don't want' 'em to get gross from the heat, if you know what I mean. Remember that in hot weather your cake frostin' will tend to melt. I suggest that you cover your cake with foil and stick it in the freezer for thirty minutes to an hour. This way, you can pull your cake out when you get to the BBQ, and by the time you're ready to eat it, it will have thawed out and not be melted all over the place. And regardless of what people might think, with heat Jell-O will melt. So keep that wonderful treat cold as well.

And for those of you in the northern part of the United States, let me explain somethin' to you about the South and desserts. You see, there's always been one dessert that every Southern woman two years of age and older has always known how to make. I don't know why, but that's just the way it is. And I should also add that it's a dish that every devout Baptist woman, regardless of what state she might live in, also knows how to make. When you're young they give you a bookmark with the Lord's Prayer on one side and an ambrosia salad recipe on the other. For those over thirteen who join the church, they get the recipe in the Baptist handbook that they get after they've been officially dunked. Now, I could have just added one recipe for this everyday treat, but with the wide variation on the topic of ambrosia, I thought it might be best to put in a few more. This way you can be the big hit at your next cookout. So get ready, 'cause here they come.

AMBROSIA SALAD

What's the difference between a Baptist and a sinner? The Baptist has a better ambrosia salad recipe.

Makes 6 servin's

1 cup mixed fruit or fruit cocktail
½ cup mandarin oranges
½ cup pineapple bits
½ cup miniature marshmallows

¾ cup dairy sour cream

¼ cup maraschino cherries, halved

¼ cup red seedless grapes

Drain the fruits well. Combine all the ingredients and mix well. Chill well.

—*Dottie Lamb, Lot #14*

PASTOR IDA MAY BEE'S AMBROSIA SALAD

Here we go.

Makes 6 servin's

¾ cup orange, diced

2 ripe bananas, sliced

½ cup green seedless grapes, chopped up

3 tablespoons lemon juice

1 cup mayonnaise

½ cup Cool Whip

¼ cup flaked coconut

Combine the oranges, bananas, and grapes in a large bowl. Add the lemon juice and chill.

In another bowl, fold the mayonnaise into the Cool Whip. Add the chilled mixture and coconut. Mix well and chill again

—*Pastor Ida May Bee, Lot #7*

CONNIE KAY'S CRANBERRY AMBROSIA SALAD

Well, she gets a ten for addin' somethin' new.

Makes 6 servin's

1 pound cranberries

½ cup sugar

3 oranges, peeled and cubed

1 can flaked coconut
½ cup chopped pecans
2 cups miniature marshmallows
8 ounces Cool Whip

Put the cranberries in a food processor and set it on chop. Pour the mush into a large bowl and add the sugar. Mix well. Put in the fridge to set overnight.

Add the oranges, coconut, pecans, and marshmallows. Mix well. Fold in the Cool Whip. Chill.

—*Connie Kay, Lot #13*

THE REAL AMBROSIA SALAD

God bless her, this might just be the very first ambrosia salad, 'cause the Lord knows she was probably around when it was invented.

Makes 4 to 6 servin's

1 cup fruit cocktail, drained
½ cup mandarin oranges, drained
½ cup pineapple bits, drained
2 bananas, cut into cubes
½ cup miniature marshmallows
¾ cup dairy sour cream
¼ cup maraschino cherries, halved
¼ cup red seedless grapes

Put everythin' in a bowl and lightly stir till everythin' is mixed well. Chill for a few hours. Serve cold.

—*Wendy Bottom, Lot #4*

THE OFFICIAL BAPTIST AMBROSIA SALAD

I know Jerry Falwell is gonna write me a letter scoldin' me for givin' this one out.

Makes 3 to 4 servin's

1 large can fruit cocktail, drained
1 regular can pineapple chunks, drained
1 regular can clementines, drained
1 cup miniature marshmallows, melted
2 cups miniature marshmallows
1½ cups sour cream
1 cup Cool Whip
½ cup powder sugar
½ cup shredded coconut
1 cup maraschino cherries, drained

Mix it all together and place in a large plastic bowl with a lid. Shake vigorously for 1 minute. Sit down and catch your breath. Place in the fridge and leave it there overnight. Stir it once again before servin'.

—*Ruby Ann Boxcar, Lot #18*

AMBROSIA POUND CAKE

Who says ambrosia has to be a salad?

Makes 1 pound cake

1½ sticks margarine, softened
¾ cup shortenin'
1½ cups sugar
5 eggs
2 teaspoons coconut extract
3 cups all-purpose flour
½ teaspoon bakin' soda
¼ teaspoon salt

1 cup freshly squeezed orange juice
1 cup shredded coconut

Prepare your tube cake pan by greasin' and flourin' it. Set this aside.

Combine the first three ingredients. Blend well, then add the eggs one at a time, makin' sure to mix each one in real good before addin' the next one. Add the coconut extract. Set aside.

In a new bowl, combine the dry ingredients and mix well. Add 'em, alternatin' with the orange juice, to the egg mixture. Add the coconut and stir well. Pour the mixture into the prepared tube cake pan. Put your pan in a cold oven. Then turn it on and let the cake bake for 1½ hours at 325 degrees F. When it's finished bakin', turn it out immediately before allowin' it to cool.

—Buck N. Hiney, Lot #1

ANGEL OF THE LORD'S AMBROSIA BARS

With a name like that, regardless if you like ambrosia or not, if you take one, you finish it for fear of bein' struck down by a bolt of lightnin' if you don't.

Makes 6 to 8 servin's, dependin' on the size that you cut the bars

1½ cups graham cracker crumbs
⅓ cup melted margarine
½ cup sugar
½ cup chunky peanut butter
8 ounces cream cheese, softened
1 regular box vanilla instant puddin'
2 cups milk
1 regular can fruit cocktail, drained
¼ cup flaked coconut
2 cups Cool Whip

Mix together the first four ingredients. Place in a 13x9-inch cookin' pan and press it down to make a crust. Stick it in the oven and bake for 3 minutes at 375 degrees F. Take it out and set aside.

Usin' an electric mixer, combine the softened cream cheese and puddin'. Then slowly add the milk and continue to mix for 3 minutes. Add the fruit cocktail and coconut. Mix until all is well mixed. Pour into the graham cracker crust. Add the Cool Whip. Cover and chill for 4 hours. Cut into bars.

—Sister Bertha, Lot #12

MRS. BOWEEVIL'S SIMPLE AS RICKEY CHOCOLATE MOUSSE

Simple yes, but I like it too.

Makes 14 to 18 servin's, but me and my husband, Dew, can eat a whole pan by ourselves

⅓ cup margarine, melted
1¼ cups graham cracker crumbs
¾ cup sugar
⅔ cup cold water
1 envelope unflavored gelatin
8 ounces cream cheese
3 regular Hershey's milk chocolate candy bars, melted
2 ounces semisweet chocolate chips, melted
1 (14-ounce) can sweetened condensed milk
1½ teaspoons vanilla extract
1 cup Cool Whip

In a bowl, combine the melted margarine, graham cracker crumbs, and sugar. Mix well with a fork. Pour into a pie pan and press the mixture down to form a crust all around. Cover and set in the freezer while you prepare the rest of the dessert.

Take the water and add the gelatin so it can dissolve. Set aside.

Put your cream cheese in a bowl and take the mixer to it till it's nice and fluffy. Add both the melted chocolates and beat again for 3 to 5 minutes. Next add the milk and vanilla and beat once more until you got a nice smooth texture. Add the totally dissolved gelatin in the water and mix.

Add your Cool Whip and fold that in. Take your pie pan from the freezer and pour in the mousse mixture. Cover it and put in the fridge to chill for 3 to 5 hours, or overnight if you like.

—*Ruby Ann Boxcar, Lot #18*

CRUNCHY FUDGY

This is kind of like that famous candy bar, but in a square!

Makes a little over 1 pound

¼ cup margarine
1 (6-ounce) package semisweet chocolate chips
¼ cup light corn syrup
1⅓ cups powdered sugar
2⅓ cups crispy rice cereal

In a big pot, melt the margarine over a medium heat. Add the chocolate chips and corn syrup, makin' sure to stir constantly. Once the chocolate chips have melted, take it off the heat. Quickly add the powdered sugar and cereal. Stir in well. Usin' a spoon or spatula, dump the mixture out from the pot into a greased square pan (9 inches is just fine in this case). Put it in the fridge to cool (30 minutes to 1 hour, dependin' on how cold your fridge is). Cut into squares.

—*Juanita Hix, Lot #9*

NEW ORLEANS–STYLE BREAD PUDDIN'

Nellie got this recipe durin' a Baptist Organist Association convention in New Orleans five years ago, which doesn't surprise me. After all, who'd know more about bourbon than a Baptist in New Orleans?

Makes 6 to 8 servin's

1 loaf French bread
1 stick margarine, melted

8 eggs
2½ cups sugar
2 cans evaporated milk
1½ teaspoons vanilla extract

Take your bread and tear it into small bits and pieces. Put it into a large bowl along with the rest of the ingredients. Mix well and pour it into a well-greased 13x9-inch foil bakin' pan. Place the pan on the grill and close the cover. Keep your BBQ at 350 degrees F. and cook for about an hour. Now the bottom of the puddin' will be very brown, but that's OK. Makin' the sauce for the puddin' is easy. You start by mixin' all the followin' in a bowl:

1 box powdered sugar
½ teaspoon vanilla extract
1 teaspoon bourbon
1½ sticks margarine, melted

If you need to thin it out, add a bit more milk or bourbon. Heat on the grill till it starts to boil and serve warm over the bread puddin'.

—*Nellie Tinkle, Lot #4*

MRS. BOWEEVIL'S YUMMY YUMMY CARROT CAKE

One whiff of this and I get weak.

Makes 1 cake

2 cups sugar
2 cups flour
2 teaspoons cinnamon
2 teaspoons bakin' soda
1 teaspoon salt
1½ cups vegetable oil
4 eggs
3 cups shredded carrots
2 teaspoons vanilla extract

1 cup chopped pecans
8 ounces cream cheese, softened
¼ pound margarine
1 pound powdered sugar

Combine the first seven ingredients together. Mix well. Add the carrots, 1 teaspoon of the vanilla, and the pecans, mixin' well also. Pour into two 9-inch floured and greased pans, and bake for 35 to 40 minutes at 350 degrees F.. Give it the old toothpick test, and if the toothpick pulls out clean when you insert it in the middle, your cake is done. Let your cakes cool down on a cake rack. In the meantime, put your cream cheese, margarine, and 1 teaspoon vanilla in a bowl and whip with a mixer till fluffy. Add the powder sugar and blend. This will be your frostin'. When the cakes are cooled down, turn them out and put a thick layer of frostin' on the top of one of the cakes. Set the second cake on top of that one and then frost 'em together to make one two-layer cake.

—Ruby Ann Boxcar, Lot #18

PEANUT BUTTER CHEESECAKE SQUARES

These are almost as good as watchin' your neighbors through a pair of binoculars.

Makes 15 squares

¼ cup margarine
⅓ cup dark brown sugar
1 cup all-purpose flour
½ cup peanut butter chips
8 ounces cream cheese, softened
¼ cup granulated sugar
1 teaspoon vanilla extract
1 egg
¾ cup M&M's

Cream the margarine and brown sugar until fluffy. Add the flour and mix well. Take half of the mixture and press into an 8-inch-square bakin' pan.

Sprinkle half the peanut butter chips on top of the mixture you just pressed in the pan. Bake for 10 to 12 minutes at 350 degrees F. Take out of oven and set aside.

In a large bowl, combine the cream cheese, sugar, ¼ cup peanut butter chips, and imitation vanilla extract. Mix well until blended. Add the egg and blend.

Take half the M&M's and sprinkle 'em over the baked crust. Put the cream cheese mixture on top of this. Mix the rest of the M&M's and peanut butter chips with the other half of the brown sugar mixture. Sprinkle on top of the cheese mixture, and bake in the oven at 350 degrees F. for 20 to 25 minutes. When it's done, take it out, let it cool completely, and cut into 15 squares.

—Harry Lombardi, Lot #19

MRS. BOWEEVIL'S MOLASSES COOKIES

I'm not big on molasses, but thanks to these, I've grown to like moles.

Makes 3 to 4 dozen cookies

¾ cup butter
¾ cup molasses
2 beaten eggs
2¼ cups flour
4 teaspoons bakin' powder
½ teaspoon bakin' soda
½ teaspoon salt
1½ teaspoons cinnamon
¼ cup milk
½ cup seedless raisins
½ cup chopped nuts

In a large bowl, cream the butter, then add the next two ingredients. Set aside. In a smaller bowl, sift the dry ingredients. Slowly alternate addin' the milk and the dry ingredients to the butter mixture. Add the raisins and nuts and stir. Roll into spoon-size balls and place on a greased cookie sheet. Take a fork and flatten each ball down. Cook for 10 to 12 minutes at 425 degrees F.

—*Ruby Ann Boxcar, Lot #18*

BBQ CAKES

I can't imagine a BBQ at the High Chaparral Trailer Park without havin' these.

Makes a dozen or so little cakes

1½ cups shortenin'
1½ cups sugar
4 large eggs, beaten
1 cup hot water
1½ cups honey
1 cup molasses
5 cups flour
3 teaspoons cinnamon
2 teaspoons bakin' soda
2 tablespoons bakin' powder

In a big bowl, cream together the shortenin' and the sugar. Mix in the eggs and add the hot water, honey, and molasses. Stir well.

In a separate bowl, combine the flour, cinnamon, bakin' soda, and bakin' powder. Slowly add to the big bowl mixture. Mix well. Cover and put in the fridge overnight. The next day, roll the dough into tablespoon-size balls and place on cookie sheet. Bake for 10 to 12 minutes at 350 degrees F. Take off of the cookie sheet and let the little cakes cool.

Eat as is or frost with your favorite icin'.

—*Lovie Birch, Lot #20*

MRS. BOWEEVIL'S LITTLE RICKEY PINEAPPLE CAKE

This is as simple as Rickey was.

Makes 1 cake

2 cups sugar
2 teaspoons bakin' soda
2 cups self-risin' flour
1 regular can crushed pineapple, with juice
2 eggs

Mix it all together and pour into a 13x9-inch ungreased pan. Stick it in the oven and let it cook for 30 to 35 minutes at 375 degrees F. Frost it with your favorite cream cheese frostin'.

—*Ruby Ann Boxcar, Lot #18*

PASTOR IDA MAY BEE'S CHERRY WHIP PIE

If you've never had this, just wait till you taste it. It's truly a blessin'.

Makes 1 pie

3 cups graham cracker crumbs
1½ cups plus ¾ cup sugar
1 cup margarine, melted
8 ounces cream cheese
1 cup milk
2 envelopes Dream Whip
2 cans cherry pie fillin'

Combine the graham cracker crumbs with the 1½ cups sugar. Make sure it is mixed well. Add the margarine and mix. It should be crumbly. Put half of this into a 9-inch pan. Press the mixture down in the bottom of the pan, just like you'd do if you was makin' a cheese cake. Cover and put in the fridge.

Cream the cream cheese and the ¾ cup sugar. Make sure that it all mixes well. Pour the milk in a large bowl followed by the Dream Whip. Whip it like it's a neighbor's kid. When it gets nice and fluffy, go ahead and add the cream cheese mixture. Continue whippin' till it gets real fluffy again. Now add the cans of cherry pie fillin' and continue whippin'. Once it's all mixed real good and is somewhat fluffy, take the pan out of the fridge and pour the mixture in it. Try to smooth it all out to where it's level and then sprinkle on the remainin' crumb mixture. Cover and put back in the fridge to chill for at least an hour.

—Pastor Ida May Bee, Lot #7

ME-MA'S CHERRY POT PIES

*As you can tell, the electroshock treatments didn't do a bit of good. Regardless of your skill at cookin', **please** don't even try to make this.*

Makes enough for a small cat

3 beef pot pies
1 can cherry pie fillin'
Super glue
3 good slices of Government cheese

Thaw out the pies. Carefully cut the top crust off. Add some cherry pie fillin' to the beefy pie. Stir. Super glue the tops back on. Put the cheese slices on each pie.

Followin' the instructions on the box, bake your pies. Serve with ice cream. Everyone likes cheese with apple pie, but I think it goes good with cherry pot pies as well.

—Me-Ma, Formerly of Lot #16

BOURBON PECAN PIE

If a piece or two of this don't make you ready for a nap, cousin, you ain't alive.

Makes 1 pie

1 Hershey's milk chocolate candy bar
1 unbaked deep-dish pie shell
3 eggs, beaten
1 cup sugar
½ teaspoon salt
⅓ cup margarine, melted
1 cup corn syrup
2 tablespoons bourbon
1 cup pecan halves

Put the candy bar in a bowl and melt in the microwave. Pour it into the pie shell. Swish the chocolate around in the shell to make sure it covers some of the side and all of the bottom. Put in the fridge to chill while you mix the remainin' ingredients.

In a large bowl, combine the next three ingredients. Fold in the margarine slowly. Mix in the corn syrup and bourbon. Mix until everything is well blended. Stir in the pecans. Pour the mixture into the shell and cover the outside of the crust with foil. Bake at 375 degrees F. for 50 minutes. Take the foil off the crust and bake another 25 minutes. Top it with a little whipped cream if you want. It's also good if you throw out the pecans and add 3 more tablespoons of bourbon.

—*Donna Sue Boxcar, Lot #6*

AUNT VIOLET'S GRAPE SALAD

Yes, this is the same Aunt Violet I mentioned in my first book, who moved to Illinois and lives in a house. She's the only family member who don't live in a trailer, and I tell y'all if this stuff wasn't so dang good, I wouldn't make it just for that reason. Oh well, I guess sometimes you just got be opened-minded, especially when food is involved.

Makes 4 to 6 servin's

2 pounds seedless red grapes
2 pounds seedless white grapes
1 cup dairy sour cream
1 (8-ounce) package of cream cheese, softened
½ cup sugar
1 teaspoon vanilla extract
3 tablespoons brown sugar

Wash the grapes and dry them good; then separate 'em from the stems.

In another bowl, mix the sour cream, cream cheese, sugar, and vanilla together. Pour this mixture over the grapes, then sprinkle with brown sugar.

—*Ruby Ann Boxcar, Lot #18*

CALVARY CANDY

Regardless of how much you've had to eat, you can always find room for some of this.

Makes about 20 pieces if cut just right

1 pound candy-makin' white chocolate
1 rounded cup of chunky peanut butter

Melt the white chocolate in microwave in a 2-cup measuring cup at 50 percent power for approximately 5 minutes, or until it's smooth. Put the peanut butter in the measurin' cup with the chocolate and stir until it is melted. Butter up an 8x8-inch dish and pour the candy into it. Refrigerate until it's set up but is not too hard. Remove from the refrigerator and cut into squares. Return to refrigerator until it gets hard.

—*Faye Faye Larue, Lot #17*

MRS. BOWEEVIL'S COOKIES

I'm leavin' for the store right now to buy milk to dunk these in!

Makes a few dozen cookies

9 eggs
2 cups brown sugar
2 cups granulated sugar
4 cups margarine
2⅔ cups peanut butter
9 cups oatmeal
16 ounces chocolate chips
12 ounces M&M's candy
2 teaspoons vanilla extract
1½ teaspoons corn syrup
4 teaspoons bakin' soda
4 teaspoons bakin' powder
8 cups all-purpose flour

Mix everythin' together and drop teaspoon-size amounts onto a cookie sheet. Bake at 350 degrees F. for 12 minutes only.

—*Ruby Ann Boxcar, Lot #18*

TACO TACKLE SHACK'S CINNAMON STRIPS

Now y'all can enjoy these without havin' to drive all the way to the Taco Tackle Shack.

Makes 50 to 60 strips

10 (8-inch) flour tortillas
1 cup granulated sugar
½ cup powdered sugar
1 teaspoon cinnamon
¼ teaspoon nutmeg
Vegetable oil for fryin' the strips

Cut the tortillas into strips. Set 'em aside.

Put all your other ingredients in a plastic freezer bag and set aside.

Get your oil hot in a skillet and put the tortillas strips in it. Fry your strips for 30 seconds on each side, or until golden brown. Drain on paper towels. While they're still warm, place the strips into the plastic bag with the other ingredients and gently shake. Make sure you get a nice coatin'. Serve!

—Lois Bunch, Lot #3

WANDA'S REAL EASY SUGAR-FREE CHOCOLATE MOUSSE

This ain't half bad for a nonsugar dessert!

Makes 4 good-size servin's

1 large box sugar-free chocolate puddin'
Heavy cream
8 ounces cream cheese, softened

Make the puddin' accordin' to the box, but use the heavy cream instead of fat-free milk. Next add the cream cheese and, usin' an electric mixer, blend on medium until it's smooth. Put in 4 cups, cover, and put in the fridge to chill.

—Wanda Kay, Lot #13

MOMMA'S BUTTERSCOTCH COOKIES

These taste as good as them little candies, but they dunk better in milk.

Makes 4 to 5 dozen cookies

½ cup shortenin'
1 teaspoon vanilla extract
1 cup dark brown sugar

1 egg
2 cups sifted flour
½ teaspoon cream of tartar
½ teaspoon salt
½ teaspoon bakin' soda
2 tablespoons milk

Thoroughly beat the shortenin', vanilla, brown sugar, and egg together in a big bowl. Set aside.

Sift the flour, cream of tartar, salt, and bakin' soda together in a separate bowl. Gradually add the flour mixture to the shortenin' mixture. Mix well. Add the milk. Mix again. Take a handful of dough and press it out with your hands into a candy bar–length piece. Place it on wax paper and continue with the rest of the dough. Place another piece of wax paper on top of each tray of dough. Put in the fridge to chill for 2 to 3 hours. Take out and cut each bar into 4 pieces. Place these pieces 1 to 1½ inches apart on a greased bakin' sheet and bake for about 7 minutes at 350 degrees F. These go real good with a big glass of milk.

—Momma Boxcar, Lot #5

Chapter 17

Tina Faye enjoys an adult beverage with her mother, Faye Faye LaRue, outside of Tina's new motel during the weekend motel BBQ. Each room is stocked with the same style of bleach bottle bar set that the gals are usin' here.

Helpful Hints

A cookbook by Ruby Ann Boxcar without a section on helpful hints would be like one of them lovemakin' manuals without pictures. Talk about bein' disappointed! This go-around I asked all the resident's of the High Chaparral to try to keep their hints on the topic of BBQin'. God bless 'em, some of 'em did stray a bit, but what the heck, by now y'all have come to expect them to be a little off anyways. Now, I did not include any helpful hints from my Me-Ma on account of the fact that even though I've warned y'all not to make the recipes that she's given me for my past two books, some of y'all ain't listened and have had to spend a few hours in your local ER. The good Lord only knows what you'd do if I gave you her helpful hints. I have a feelin' the fire department in your part of the world would be keepin' busy. So those are out!

By the way, do you have a helpful hint you'd like to share with all of us or are you just lookin' for more hints from your fellow readers? Good, then go to my Web pages at www.rubyann.org, click on the enter button, and look for the "Helpful Hints Message Board." Leave your easy tips or simply write down the ones that you like that readers have taken the time to share. And the good thing about it is that you ain't got to even have an e-mail to give us your tips. So you can even go to your local library and use their computers to access the helpful hints and even add your own. Ain't that great! So please sign on and have fun.

So without any further ado, here they are (the helpful hints, not the lovemakin' pictures).

HINTS LOT BY LOT

- You can easily slice round steak when it's partially frozen.
- Wrap the outside of the pans you'll be usin' on the BBQ with heavy-duty aluminum foil. This will stop your pans from gettin' all black from the fire. When you're done, just take off the foil and throw it away.
- Before you cook your meat, rinse the meat with hot water, then pat it down with a dry paper towel. This will not only cleanse your meat, but it will also prepare it to hold in the spices and/or seasonin's you're about to apply.
- Serve and eat your items that you take off the BBQ as soon as possible, 'cause if you don't, they will continue to cook and dry out.
- If you have to warm up a cooked meat item on the grill, brush some margarine or BBQ sauce on it, wrap it up with lettuce leaves, and then put it on the BBQ via a grill wok or grill topper. This will keep the meat moist.

> —*Opal Lamb-Inman, Lot #1*
> —*Dick Inman, Lot #1*
> —*Uri Krochichin, Lot #1*
> —*Buck N. Hiney, Lot #1*

- Instead of usin' wood chunks, which can cost and arm and a leg, go to your local school and ask if you can take some of their sawdust from their shop class. They'd love to give it to you. Then all you got to do is sprinkle it over your fire when you're cookin', for that great wood flavor.
- Don't throw away those empty pickle jars from the BBQ. Instead, combine all the juices in one jar and store in your fridge. The pickle juice is great when mixed with salad dressin's or even added to potato salad.
- If you want to toast bread on your BBQ, take two pieces of bread at a time, butter one side of each slice, and put the buttered sides together. Place the combined bread on the grill tray or grill wok and toast both dry sides. You'll end up with two pieces of toast with a nice crisp outside and a warm juicy inside.
- Before usin' those peas for a pea salad, add a Worcestershire sauce for an even better flavor.

- Put your used margarine wrappers in a plastic bag and keep in the fridge. These are great when you got to grease a pan.
—*Anita Biggon, Lot #2*

- When usin' a grill tray, grill wok, or even a grill basket, take the food off of 'em as soon as they've finished cookin'. If you take the tray or wok off the BBQ with the food on it, and set it aside, the food will still continue to cook even though the grill tray and grill wok are not in contact with the BBQ anymore. If you leave your food item in the grill basket, it, too, will continue to cook from the heated basket wires.
- Spread a thick layer of margarine over the cut edges of avocados to stop 'em from turnin' black.
- Before servin' gravies at your next BBQ, whip 'em up with an egg beater. This will help to avoid a filmy coatin' on the surface.
- If you're short an egg when it comes time to make a recipe that calls for an egg to hold it together, such as a hamburger patty, substitute one package of dissolved gelatin.
- When cookin' veggies, the golden rule is that you cover those vegetables that are grown underground, and don't cover those that are grown above ground.
—*Lois Bunch, Lot #3*
—*Hubert Bunch, Lot #3*

- Place lettuce that needs to be freshened up in a large bowl with cold water and the juice of one lemon.
- Tired of havin' to oil and then flour cake pans? Simply combine 1 cup of Crisco (melted), 1 cup of vegetable oil, and 1 cup of flour with an electric mixer. Place in a container with a lid and keep in the fridge. When you need to oil and flour your pans, just use a little bit of this instead.
- Before applyin' your dry rubs, coat your meat with a thin layer of mustard.
- Got extra BBQ'd meat left over? Freeze it for later.
- My husband's meat always tastes better if he waits to put a little BBQ sauce on it after he's finished cookin' it. He slaps a little sauce on it, then

moves it over to the part of the BBQ that is the coolest. He turns it after a minute and gets it off quickly.

—CM Tinkle, Lot #4
—Nellie Tinkle, Lot #4
—Wendy Bottom, Lot #4

- I like to take an onion and chop it up into big pieces, mix it with 2 tablespoons of olive oil, and wrap it in foil. I then place it on the fire when I'm cookin' my meats. If you close the lid, that wonderful smell will get into your meat for a taste sensation. After you finish the cookin', take the wrapped onion out and enjoy it as well.
- If you take fresh-peeled garlic and slowly add it to your food processor along with just enough water to keep it goin', you will get a nice puréed substance that you can pour into small freezer bags. Just put a little in each bag and lay 'em on their sides. Once the purée freezes, you should have a thin flat layer in each bag. Open up the bags and force the air out, then reseal 'em. Now when you need garlic for a recipe, all you got to do is break off a chunk and you got fresh garlic all year round.
- A light layer of oil on your chicken will help to keep on that dry rub. Also, if you slide your fingers between the chicken skin without tearin' it, you can sprinkle some of that rub in there as well. This makes for a very flavorful cooked chicken.

—Momma Boxcar, Lot #5
—Daddy Boxcar, Lot #5

- When cookin' with liquor, make sure you always have twice the amount on hand than the recipe calls for. Nothin' is worse than not havin' enough booze for your food just because you got a little parched while preparin' a dish.
- If your salad or dessert lights up and flambés 'cause it got too close to the BBQ, don't worry. Simply cover it with foil until it goes out, move three or four feet away from the BBQ and pour more liquor over the food item. Stir.
- When flambéin' a dish, never, never, never ever use the good booze.

- Soakin' your BBQ utensils in a large bowl of vodka for a few minutes will guarantee that they're exceptionally clean and free of germs. Feel free to lick each one dry after takin' 'em out of the bowl. Why waste paper towels?
- You can never have enough ice on hand durin' those long hot summer months.

—Donna Sue Boxcar, Lot #6

- Never chop vegetables on the same cuttin' board that you used for meat unless you've sanitized it first.
- You never know when the Lord will move you to BBQ, so keep plenty of propane on hand. If you ain't got a gas grill, then I will keep you in my prayers, but in the meantime, brothers and sisters, keep lots of extra bags of charcoal on hand and in a dry place.
- After you've removed your meat from the marinade, make sure you pat it dry with a paper towel. This will make sure that it cooks evenly on the BBQ.
- Never put frozen meat on the grill. By the time the middle is finished the outside will look like it went to hell and back. Trust me when I tell y'all, it ain't pretty.
- Do your best not to lift the lid unless it's to test the temperature of the BBQin' item. The more often you lift the lid, the longer it takes for it to cook. Don't be nosy.

—Pastor Ida May Bee, Lot #7
—Brother Woody Bee, Lot #7

- Keep lots of ice in your freezer, 'cause you never know when your aunt is gonna desperately need it.
- Never leave children, dogs, or chicken in a hot car.
- Take the chicken out of the fridge only when you are ready to put it on the grill or you will get real real sick and feel like you're about to die and go to heaven.
- Never put uncooked chicken and soft drinks in the same cooler or you will get real sick again and feel like you are gonna die again.
- Let somebody else cook the chicken.

—Lulu Bell Boxcar, Lot #8

- When attendin' BBQs, put your condiments in small containers rather than cartin' along the whole bottles.
- All foods should be eaten within two hours after they've been cooked.
- Coolers are great for storin' either cold food or hot food.
- Make sure that you chill your food thoroughly before placin' it in a cooler. This will help to keep it cool.
- Regardless of what anyone tells you, bowlin' and drinkin' do not mix.
  —Juanita Hix, Lot #9
  —Harland Hix, Lot #9

- Keep a small clock close to the grill so you can easily keep track of your cookin' time.
- When you marinate your meats, place the meats in a plastic bag and then add the marinade. This will ensure that you don't use more marinade than you need. Store the unused mixture in a container in the fridge.
- When BBQin' chicken that calls for a sauce to go over it, cook the chicken until it's halfway done, then add the sauce. This will stop your sauce from burnin' onto the chicken.
- Press a thumb print into the middle of each hamburger on both sides of the meat when you BBQ it. This helps stop the meat from swellin' up in the middle when you cook it.
- Keep old salt containers. You can easily refill 'em with your favorite rubs.
  —Ollie White, Lot #10

- A washed-out beer bottle makes a great container for your BBQ sauces or marinades. Just cover the top with foil and a tight rubber band to seal it shut.
- Reheat leftovers until they're warm in the middle.
- Wrapped-up pork will last in the fridge for four days.
- Before cuttin' onions, spear a piece of bread about an inch long and wide on the end of your knife. The bread will absorb all the fumes that make you cry.
- When cuttin' cheese, stick your knife over the BBQ grill till it gets nice and warm. This will make your cheese cuttin' a pleasure for all.
  —Kitty Chitwood, Lot #11
  —Kyle Chitwood, Lot #11

- If you write your name real big on the inside of all your containers, then when the food is taken, everyone can see that you were the one who made it.
- When handling raw fish, stick your hands in ice-cold water first. Chillin' your hands first will stop the odor from absorbin' into your skin.
- Keep your lemons covered with water in mason jars. They will last for months.
- Keep your foods covered with lids or with foil until it's time to eat.
- To ensure that your food is good, always have the person that goes to church every Sunday say the blessin'. God will listen to their prayers first 'cause he knows who they are.

 —Sister Bertha, Lot #12

- When you find a good deal on hamburger or hot dog buns and buy several bags, rather than freezin' 'em by the bag, sort 'em out into two buns per freezer bag and put 'em in the freezer. This way you don't have to thaw out more than you need at a time.
- If you find a real good price on hamburger meat, form it into patties, place 'em on wax paper, lay 'em out in a single layer on a cookie sheet, and stick 'em in the freezer. Once the patties freeze, you can stack 'em up on top of each other and wrap 'em up. They won't stick together if they're done this way.
- Keep your sugar in a salt shaker. This is handy when you need to add a little to a dish out by the BBQ.
- When a recipe is doubled, never double the spices or the salt unless it's a rub or a marinade. If it's a sauce, taste the double batch and then decide if you need more spice.
- If you use a kitchen timer out by your BBQ, set it to ring a minute or two before the actual time. That way if you're doin' somethin' else, you can quickly finish it up and still turn your meat in time.

 —Mickey Ray Kay, Lot #13
 —Connie Kay, Lot #13
 —Wanda Kay, Lot #13

- Take your hard-as-a-rock brown sugar and moisten it with water. Stick it in the microwave and cook on high until it dissolves. Add a few drops of vanilla extract, maple flavorin', and liquid smoke. Add a little ketchup and use as a bastin' sauce.
- When your recipe calls for chopped onion, as long as it ain't for grilled onion, simply grate it instead. It really adds that onion flavor into your dish.
- When shapin' hamburger patties, use wet hands. This makes the job faster and easier.
- Next time when you're makin' individual salads for a BBQ, put the salad dressin' in each bowl first followed by the croutons or boiled eggs or little tomatoes. Then add the lettuce. This'll make sure that the lettuce stays crisp until each person is ready to eat their salad.
- You can get rid of those stains on your stainless steel by usin' a scourin' pad dipped in an ammonia and water solution. If that don't work, add a little abrasive cleaner to the stainless steel and then use the scourin' pad soaked in ammonia and water. That should do the trick.

    —Dottie Lamb, Lot #14
    —Ben Beaver, Lot #14

- Take half-gallon milk cartons and cut 'em down so they stand four inches tall. Pour your drippin' cans from your BBQs into these milk carton sections so they are about three-fourths of the way full. Add wild bird seed, stir, and put in freezer. When winter comes along you can punch small holes in the top of the carton sections, run a string through the holes, and hang these in the trees for emergency cold-weather food for wild birds.
- When you get tired of those leftover hamburger patties, break 'em up into pieces, add ½ cup ketchup, ½ cup crushed crackers, ½ cup chopped onions, 2½ teaspoons salt, 2 teaspoons Worcestershire sauce, and 1 can of condensed tomato soup to make a grand diva–style meat sauce.
- When it's your turn to provide the plates for the dessert and coffee part of the BBQ, simply make it easy for yourself by puttin' the good china cups and saucers, sugar and cream bowls, and the dessert plates on a

large tray. This way when it's time for dessert, you can carry these items to the picnic table in one elegant trip.

- If you wrap the bottom of your soda pop bottles and cans with foil, they will stay cooler much longer once you take 'em out of the cooler.
- When you clean your gas grill, you can get to those hard-to-reach places like behind the dials with a cotton swab dipped in dish detergent.

—Donny Owens, Lot #15
—Kenny Lynn, Lot #15

- For goodness sake, listen to Donna Sue and always have tons and tons of ice around your trailer.
- Save those pot pie dishes to put leftover food items in. If you save the plastic lids from your two-pound coffee cans as well, they will fit the pot pie dishes perfectly. You can also stack each dish on top of the other in the fridge. This saves you lots of room.
- An old piece of corrugated cardboard covered in foil makes the perfect stove mat for the BBQ. You can place your hot dishes on this and if it should blow away when nothin's settin' on it, you ain't out anythin' but the cost of the foil.
- Always wrap yourself in a flame-retardant pup tent if you're goin' to drink alcohol close to a lit BBQ. Make sure to wear oven mitts at all times as well. This may sound too hot to wear durin' those miserable summer months, but trust me and what's left of my eyebrows, it can get a heck of a lot hotter if you don't.
- Since you never know when a light breeze might knock you over durin' these BBQs, don't break your good glassware. A two-pound coffee can makes the perfect margarita glass. Just salt the rim and watch out for jagged edges.

—Momma Ballzak, Lot #16

- If for some reason beyond my imagination, you run out of ice trays (I got forty full and in my freezer at all times), then use plastic egg containers. Just make sure you clean them out first.
- Don't throw out those old laundry soap bottles. Instead clean 'em out *real* well and fill 'em with whiskey sours or your favorite pitcher of mixed

drinks. These are great for outdoor use, but make sure you mark the bottles clearly. There is nothin' like expectin' a swig of a vodka stinger and gettin' a mouthful of soap.

- Bend the prongs on an old fork so they are halfway bent out. This is great for gettin' pickles out of a jar, and durin' the BBQ, you can hang the fork from the lip of the pickle jar.
- Can't get the cork out of that bottle? Just wrap a hot towel around the neck of the bottle, and as the heat makes the glass openin' expand, the cork will loosen and come right out.
- Don't salt your meat when BBQin' until your meat is nearly done.
  —*Faye Faye Larue, Lot #17*
  —*Tina Faye Stopenblotter, Lot #17*

- Always sear the outside of your meats first. Then reduce your heat and move the meats over to a cooler part of your BBQ to cook until the grill cools down a bit. This'll guarantee a juicier piece of meat.
- Regardless if you use wood chips or sawdust to add flavor to your meat, you need to make sure they've been soaked or dampened in water, beer, or some kind of substance before bein' put on the fire.
- Avoid custard- or cream-filled desserts for BBQs on account of 'em spoilin' quickly. If you keep 'em in your trailer fridge till it's time for dessert, then bring 'em out for fast consumption, that's just fine. Otherwise, forget about servin' 'em.
- When you go out to buy your groceries at the Piggly Wiggly, write out your shoppin' list on an envelope first. Then put all your coupons you'll be usin' in that envelope and seal it up. This way you are sure to have a fast and easy checkout at the store.
- Don't handle your hamburger meat very much when shapin' the patties. It's a lot like dough, and will become firm and heavy when it's cooked.
  —*Rubby Ann Boxcar, Lot #18*
  —*Dew Ballzak, Lot #18*

- As we all know, BBQs and most any social gatherin' can cause headaches. If this happens, take half a lime and rub it on your head. The throbbin' will go away. Of course if you're not careful, the juice will get in your eyes and they'll burn like a marshmallow on a stick.

- Pour the leftover wine from that day's BBQ in ice trays and put it in the freezer. Then when you have that unscheduled date over, you can simple pull out a cube for you and a cube for her.
- For quick relief from mosquito bites, rub soap on 'em. If you can't reach all those bites, duct tape a bar onto a stick and get to soapin'.
- When wearin' a Speedo to a BBQ, be careful of wooden benches. Not only can they break under large amounts of weight, but you can also easily get splinters. If the latter is the case, grab some Scotch tape and place it over the splinter. Scotch tape will usually pull out almost all splinters as well as body hair.
- Regardless of how much body hair you might have, always wear a shirt and pants when BBQin'. Let people find one little curly hair in their food and they'll blame you for the rest of your life.

    —Vance Pool, Lot #19
    —Harry Lombardi, Lot #19
    —Elroy Dasafe, Lot #19

- When reheatin' chicken, make sure it is covered to ensure that it's heated all the way through.
- If you're usin' gravy at your BBQ, bring a pan that can be placed on the grill. You will want to bring that gravy to a rollin' boil before servin' to make sure that all the bacteria it might have gathered when it cooled off is killed and the gravy's safe to consume.
- Treat pork and even beef just like you would chicken when it comes to handlin' it.
- To make those hamburgers cook faster, punch a few holes clean through in the middle with a toothpick before placin' the patties on the BBQ. The middle section will cook quicker.
- Try to turn your hamburgers only once and never flatten 'em. You'll lose all that good inside juice if you do.

    —Lovie Birch, Lot #20
    —Elmer Birch, Lot #20

Index